PENNSYLVANIA CONSTITUTIONAL DEVELOPMENT

PENNSYLVANIA CONSTITUTIONAL DEVELOPMENT

By ROSALIND L. BRANNING
Associate Professor of Political Science
University of Pittsburgh

UNIVERSITY OF PITTSBURGH PRESS

Library of Congress Card Catalog Number: 59-15246

© 1960, University of Pittsburgh Press

Printed in the United States of America

To Elmer Diedrich Graper
— scholar, great teacher, devoted public servant —
this book is dedicated
by one who has been privileged to know him as
a teacher, department head, and friend.

CONTENTS

Introduction 1

PART ONE: CONSTITUTIONAL DEVELOPMENT

Chapter 1. Pennsylvania's Liberal Constitution of 1776.... 9

Chapter 2. Pennsylvania's Conservative Constitution of 1790 17

Chapter 3. Pennsylvania's Compromise Constitution of 1838 21

PART TWO: PENNSYLVANIA'S REFORM CONSTITUTION OF 1874

Chapter 4. Economic, Social, and Political Setting, 1874.... 37

Chapter 5. The Calling of the Convention of 1872-1873.... 55

Chapter 6. Work of the Constitutional Convention: Legislative, Executive, Judiciary.............. 59

Chapter 7. Chains for the Giants: Political Machines, Corporations, Railroads 87

Chapter 8. Battle for Ratification of the Reform Constitution 109

Chapter 9. An Evaluation of the Reform Constitution...... 123

PART THREE: TWENTIETH CENTURY DEVELOPMENTS

Chapter 10. Twentieth Century Growth 127

Chapter 11. Amendment or Revision? 147

Bibliography 157

Index 161

ERRATUM

While this volume was in printing the General Assembly approved a conference report on House Bill 1977, implementing the Absentee Ballot amendment (see page 144).

Governor Lawrence signed the Act on January 8, 1960.

INTRODUCTION

A biographer must of necessity decide how far into the past it is essential to go in tracing the ancestral line of the person whose biography he is writing, so that he may give his readers a fair understanding of the inheritance and the cultural setting from which his hero has sprung, yet not weary them with too many generations of disinterred ancestors. And so, likewise, in tracing the constitutional lineage of a state, the author must decide at what point to begin in the unbroken political growth of a community. Certainly the experience of Pennsylvania under its colonial frames of government, especially the Charter of Privileges, contributed markedly to subsequent constitutional developments during Pennsylvania's statehood. Nor may one ignore the influence of its English political and legal heritage, the challenge of Whig political philosophy, and more particularly the political and social ideas of the Great Proprietor. In a monograph whose major purpose is a critical analysis of the present constitution of Pennsylvania as a tool for the study of the problems springing from the rigidity of its provisions, an extended excursion into historical origins is impossible. The author has for this reason confined the historical portions of this monograph to constitutional development relating to the framing of the state constitutions of 1776, 1790, 1838, and 1874, and has omitted any exposition of the colonial frames of government.

Of the four fundamental documents, the constitution of 1874 has proved the most enduring. Its survival for more than three-quarters of a century, however, can scarcely be attributed to such qualities of breadth and flexibility as have rendered the national Constitution workable under the pressures of twentieth-century social and economic changes. Indeed, so many amendments have been added that the resulting patchwork would rival the patched garments of a medieval mendicant! In spite of such amendments and some letting out of the seams the constitutional garment has been outgrown as the commonwealth has reached mid-twentieth-century maturity. The question of constitutional revision has been a persistent issue, with recurrent pledges by parties and candidates for governorship bringing recurrent hope and disappointment. Constitutional commissions have been appointed by several governors, but their well-considered recommendations have failed to bear fruit. Five times the people of Pennsylvania have been given an opportunity to authorize the calling of a constitutional convention, but each time they have rejected it. The 1957 session of the General Assembly authorized the appointment of a commission on constitutional revision. If these renewed efforts toward revision are to be more successful than those of the past it seems self-evident that the public must be educated to the need for constitutional change, that the misunderstandings and misapprehensions (often encouraged by interested groups not wishing to forego advantages bulwarked by the present document) must be dispelled.

The urgent need for constitutional change cannot be satisfied by the addition of a few more amendments. The need springs out of the very nature of the present constitution. It is not simply that the Pennsylvania constitution is old—the national Constitution is much older; not simply that it is tediously long, though it is three times the length of the constitution of 1838; not primarily because it contains some articles which hardly attain the dignity of constitutional provisions; nor even because in part it is expressed in archaic language. Pennsylvania needs a new constitution because the convention which drafted the present one, in its earnest zeal to promote good government, so hampered the legislature that it cannot act efficiently or effectively. It needs a new constitution because the then prevailing conceptions of a rural society are frozen into the provisions for the judiciary and for county government. It needs a new constitution because the constitution of 1874 is in many respects inflexible and unadaptable to modern needs. Above all, it needs a new constitution because the framers of the constitution failed to grasp fully the difference between constitutional and statutory law, and therefore have produced a document which defies the basic principles of good draftsmanship.

Since the framing of the constitution the population of Pennsylvania has grown from four to ten and a half million, and its budget has mounted from seven million to approximately a billion per annum. The constitution guarantees at least one million dollars a year for support of public schools, but during the current biennium the state is spending almost three quarters of a billion for public education! Appropriations for highways and public assistance, the other major items in the present day state budget, had not yet found their way into state expenditures when the constitution-makers agreed upon the financial provisions in the present document. In that pre-automobile age, uncomplicated by super-highways and city parkways, there was no need for a state highway system, or even for state aid to local governments for highway purposes. Welfare and health functions were most rudimentary.

With the growth in functions which has taken place during the present century the state legislature has been hard pressed to find new ways to meet rising costs. It has been subjected to strong pressures, also, to assume an increasing share of the costs of local government. In dealing with the complex problems facing it the legislature is handicapped by limitations on its taxing power, especially by its inability to levy a graduated personal income tax; limitations upon its power to borrow; its lack of authority to pass special legislation; and its inability to deal constructively with county government. It can neither simplify the structure of government in rural counties nor combine those counties which are too small to support a separate county government. It cannot reorganize the structure of government in large counties along the lines of conformity with best modern practices for efficiency in management. It can deal with the special problems of metropolitan counties only by the awkward device of constitutional amendment. Limitations on powers which make it impossible for the legislature to make decisions in the terms of the best solution tend to encourage irresponsibility in action.

The provision for biennial sessions has also tended to weaken the legislature. In 1873 it seemed quite reasonable to assume that the legislature, freed from the burden of special legislation, could handle all the necessary legislation at a brief meeting in alternate years. One glance at the huge volume necessary to publish the session laws of a current legislative session is sufficient to dispel such false notions today! The enormous growth in the volume and variety of legislation, and more especially the growth in the size of the budget have made annual sessions imperative. The present system has weakened legislative control over the budget. With biennial sessions have come biennial budgets. A biennial budget necessitates the forecasting of the financial program for a two-year period, with resultant inaccuracies. Each biennium the legislature is asked by the governor to pass deficiency appropriations, sometimes amounting to thirty or forty million dollars. The newly adopted amendment providing for annual sessions, with the session in the even-numbered years limited to action on the budget, should be an improvement in this regard. It is unfortunate, however, that the second session is so limited, forcing the consideration of the budget in a policy vacuum rather than in the context of the policy program of which it is a part. An unlimited continuing session would have been wiser.

Many of the provisions respecting procedure are outworn. They not only are no longer necessary, but they are time-consuming and costly. The provision requiring the reading of all bills at length on three separate days in each house, for example, imposes a requirement which is ridiculous and impossible. The volume of legislation handled would make a single reading at length time-consuming; certainly no useful purpose could be served by reading bills at length six times over when every bill is printed and placed on the desk of each member after it is reported out of committee. Actually bills are never read at length, though time is wasted in a meaningless ritual in which a polite gesture toward compliance is substituted. This tends to create the unwarranted impression in the public mind that the whole legislative process is farcical, and thus to lower the stature of the legislative body in the public eye. The printing of the bills at length in the legislative journal for each of the readings is costly. More important, though, is the fact that in an emergency—as in the banking and insurance crisis in 1933—delay may bring disaster so that a choice must be made between strict compliance with the fundamental document and a betrayal of public interest. The requirement that no bill shall contain more than one subject, though designed with an understandable purpose, has tended to discourage the passage of codes and needlessly to multiply the number of laws passed.

This is by no means a complete catalogue of the ways in which our legislature is hampered by constitutional strictures, but is indicative of the handicaps under which it struggles. Certainly the legislative body should be competent to establish its own rules of procedure. A broadening of its powers would place it in a much better position to fulfill its obligations to the people. A far better check than the artificial limitations imposed by a constitutional convention, which spoke in the terms of the problems of its day, would be the more natural democratic check of continuous public scrutiny. Modern systems of publicity under the watchful eyes of the press render improbable a return to the evils which provoked the imposition of the constitutional safeguards. We should remember that the same limitations which are designed to prevent a legislative body from injuring the public interest operate to prevent it from promoting public interest.

All that has thus far been said in respect to its shortcomings is in a very real sense comprehended in the statement that our present constitution is based upon a misconception of the nature of the fundamental law which we call a constitution. The men who framed our constitution apparently did not perceive the difference between the respective purposes served by constitutional and statutory law. The former, the constitution, sets down the basic principles in regard to the distribution of functions among the branches of government (executive, legislative, and judicial), the distribution of powers between the central government and local units of government (or, perhaps, the concentration of authority at the central level, as is commonly true in state constitutions), and the relationship between the government and its people. It determines the degree to which the people may participate in their government, and in a legal sense who are "the people" who thus take part in the political life of the community. It provides for the measure of responsibility of the government toward its people. It both reflects the political, social, and ethical concepts and aspirations of the people it governs, and conditions the future development of the political community. It may serve as a guide and strong anchor in times of turbulence and stress, or as a hindrance in the normal adjustment to changes in political and social needs. Whether it guides or hinders depends upon the political judgment or the narrowness of vision of those who serve as its architects.

Statutory law, on the other hand, serves as the means by which the government, within the framework of the fundamental constitutional concepts, deals with the myriad of problems, often swiftly changing ones, confronting society. It is necessarily more transitory than constitutional law. The legislature, representing the people, must undertake new functions and services as required by changed conditions, and abandon those no longer useful; it must adapt the rules and regulations by which it promotes and protects public interest to the needs of an increasingly complex society; it must create the governmental agencies to perform public services and enforce regulations; and it must provide the financial means to support governmental programs. All this is accomplished through statutory law, which can be changed or repealed by simple legislative act. Flexibility and adaptability are indispensable, not only from the point of view of progressive development in adjustment to social and economic changes, but also from the point of view of democratic responsibility. It is through the changes in major legislative programs that the changes in popular will as expressed in popular elections are mirrored. In the midst of change the constitution serves as a unifying factor, setting the general conceptual framework within which statutory development takes place, and giving continuity to the political life of the society.

Properly balanced the constitution and statutory law thus reconcile the twin principles of permanence of fundamental concepts and a nice adjustment of the law to contemporary needs. If, however, the constitutional architects embody within the written constitution material of a statutory nature, the balance is destroyed. With the passage of time many of the provisions are certain to become unsuited to new conditions. The imposition of the will of a past generation upon the present is not only unwise but undemocratic.

Probably as a consequence of the convention's absorption with legislative matters, the chief executive escaped most of the hampering limitations on executive authority which generally were written into state constitutions of that era. In the main, constitutional provisions have not served as a bar to the development of effective executive control through administrative direction and fiscal supervision of administrative departments. The really serious defect in the executive article is its proscription of a successive term for the governor. The direct effect of this provision is the weakening of the governor's legislative leadership during the second session of the General Assembly, and the lowering of the prestige of the governorship, itself. Removal of this limitation would not only strengthen his position in the policy-making field, but also increase the pressure for responsible executive action, especially in the budgetary field.

The Chesterman commission has pointed out the desirability of certain additional changes in this article.

The trail blazed by New Jersey in its constitutional reorganization of the judiciary spotlights many weak points in our own judiciary article. Court delays and backlogs in the courts of record point to the need for modernization of our court structure and procedure. The survival of the untrained, politically chosen, fee compensated justice of peace court in mid-twentieth century urban society is an anomaly.

This is by no means a complete catalogue of the defects in the present constitution, but sufficient to indicate the urgency of revision. It is sufficient, also, to indicate the necessity for a breadth of vision and liberality of spirit on the part of future constitution-makers lest they, with burning zeal for reform, create anew the problem of rigidity by writing into a new constitution detailed reform provisions, especially in the area of administrative and judicial structure.

PART ONE

Constitutional Background

CHAPTER 1: PENNSYLVANIA'S LIBERAL CONSTITUTION OF 1776

No Pennsylvania constitution was framed under more dramatic circumstances than the constitution of 1776, drafted by a convention meeting in Philadelphia at a time when the brave tones of Liberty Bell had scarcely ceased to reverberate through the city, when Continental soldiers and British troops were locked in uncertain struggle, and rumors of impending invasion of the capital city were daily conversation. But the story of the constitution of 1776 does not really begin with the assembling of convention delegates in mid-July of that historic year. It had its beginning in events apparently remote from the problems of constitution making, events as varied as the shifting tides of immigration to colonial Pennsylvania, the change in religious profession of the successors of the Great Proprietor, Indian ravages along the frontier during the early days of the French and Indian War, and the growing political consciousness of disfranchised groups. The convention which framed Pennsylvania's first state constitution does, indeed, mark the culmination of a political movement that ousted from control the upper-class eastern leadership which had dominated in colonial affairs, a movement whose roots lay deep in the political controversies resulting from sectional, social, economic, and religious differences in colonial Pennsylvania.

At the mid-century sectional differences were clearly discernible.[1] In the East the three original counties of Philadelphia, Chester, and Bucks (erected by the Great Proprietor) and the city of Philadelphia were inhabited mainly by the English of Quaker, Episcopalian, and Baptist faiths. Here the Quakers and others of the wealthy merchant

---
[1]Edward Channing, *The History of the United States* (New York, 1927), III, 196-97.

class held the dominant position. In Philadelphia City the Quakers were greatly outnumbered, but strict naturalization provisions and the £50 property qualification for voting reduced the political importance of non-Quaker elements. Significantly, Philadelphia was assigned only about one-fourth as many representatives in the Assembly as it should have had under a system of equitable representation on the basis of population.

The middle counties were settled largely by German farmers of Reformed or Lutheran religious conviction. They were a thrifty, industrious people who reaped a comfortable living from the fertile valleys. They were not, however, as prosperous as the ruling merchants in the East. In politics, throughout most of the colonial period, they followed the leadership of the Quakers.

The West, on the other hand, was inhabited mainly by Scotch-Irish Presbyterians, who were for the most part small farmers, often struggling under the burden of debt. Here, as in the city of Philadelphia, the property qualification excluded large numbers from political participation. Here, likewise, the device of underrepresentation was used by the ruling eastern oligarchy to prevent any shift in political power in the Assembly. The three eastern counties, with a population scarcely greater than that of the western counties, had more than double the number of representatives.

Pennsylvania emerged from the French and Indian War with political differences sharpened. The Scotch-Irish frontiersman, whose desperate appeals for assistance had gone unheeded in the early days of the war when Indians burned their homes and scalped their kinsmen, now demanded fair representation in the Assembly. Their chief opponents were the Quakers and their German allies, who formed the Anti-Proprietary Party. The Quakers, who had been alienated from the proprietors when the proprietors accepted the Anglican faith, now demanded taxation of the proprietary estates, and even abolition of the proprietorship. To this they added opposition to the demands of the backwoodsmen. Leaders of the Proprietary Party, seeing an opportunity to strengthen their position by forming an alliance with the West, took up the cause of the frontiersmen. Composed initially of Anglicans and Presbyterians in the East, the Proprietary Party, as its name implied, defended the rights of the proprietor. The Anglicans had become vigorous champions of the Penns after their abandonment of the Quaker faith. The eastern Presbyterians, like the new members of the alliance in the West, cared little for the Penns, but were glad to enter an alliance against the Quakers. They were glad, likewise, to support the proprietor because of the growing hostility toward the Crown; the continuance of the proprietorship was regarded as preferable to the conversion of Pennsylvania into a royal colony.

The years between the French and Indian War and the convention of 1776 were years that witnessed the swift rush of events that ultimately led to war and independence. In Pennsylvania the revolutionary movement placed heavy strains upon political alliances, both old and new. The Quakers were willing to seek redress of grievances by peaceful means; they denounced the oppressive acts of Parliament, but their religious scruples forbade participation in war and revolution or the recognition of a revolutionary government established by extra-legal means. Their longtime allies, the Germans, remained faithful to their leadership until after the Declaration of Independence, then rallied to the revolutionary cause.

The majority of the Episcopalians, many of them leaders in the social, economic, and commercial life of the colony, were Loyalists and soon broke away from their alliance with the West. The Scotch-Irish in the frontier counties, in contrast, were almost unanimous in their support of the patriot cause. They were soon joined in a new political alliance by the disfranchised element in the East, which was stoutly promoting colonial resistance. Extra-legal committees of safety and provincial conferences were elected. Since no property qualifications were required for participants in this revolutionary action, the bodies selected were far more radical than the provincial Assembly.

Made more bold by their revolutionary activities, the radical elements began to urge upon the Assembly many important reforms: reapportionment of representation, liberalization of the naturalization requirements, and abolition of the oath of allegiance to England. Frightened by such revolutionary action, the conservatives of the East sought to save their position of control by making concessions to radical demands. They granted a reapportionment of representation, assigning thirty seats to the East and twenty-eight to the West. This was still unfair to the rapidly growing West, whose population now outnumbered the East.

The Assembly, however, was never able to keep pace with the revolutionary movement; radical elements in both East and West grew impatient with half-way measures and urged the drafting of a new constitution. When in November, 1775, the Assembly instructed the Pennsylvania delegation in Continental Congress to reject any proposal for separation from England, the radical group was completely alienated. During the long winter months that followed, the revolutionary temper quickened with the continuance of military conflict, and the gulf between the conservative Assembly and the revolutionary leaders widened.

On May 15, 1776, Continental Congress suggested the adoption of constitutions by colonies where "no government sufficient to the exigencies of their affairs" had been established; five days later it urged the suppression of all government under the Crown and the substitution of government based upon the will of the people. On the same day the Committee of Correspondence of Philadelphia, under the leadership of the radical element, issued a call to the committees of correspondence of the counties for a provincial conference. When the conference met at Carpenters Hall on June 24 and 25, 1776, the radicals were again in control, and they promptly put through a resolution calling for a constitutional convention. Since the resolution[2] providing for this revolutionary constitutent assembly assigned to each county and to the city of Philadelphia equal representation, and enfranchised all taxpayers and small property holders, while excluding from voting persons "suspected or publicly denounced as enemies to the liberties of America" (unless they publicly abjured allegiance to the Crown), the radicals were assured of control of the proposed convention. The conference also unanimously declared in favor of a declaration of independence.

Once more the Assembly attempted to stay the tide of revolutionary action by making last minute concessions. The naturalization requirements were swept aside, the oath of allegiance to Great Britain abolished, and the instructions withdrawn which had forbidden Pennsylvania delegates to Continental Congress to accept any declaration of independence. The radical movement, however, had already gone too far to be turned aside by such concessions. When the Assembly realized this, it considered calling a rival convention with eastern supremacy preserved, but finally gave up this proposal lest such action should lead to anarchy.[3]

It was not an easy question thus proposed to the Pennsylvania voters. Should they cast aside the time-honored Charter of Privileges which had served them for three-quarters of a century? It is true that the disfranchised had grown restless under the voting restrictions, and

---

[2]Sherman Day, *Historical Collections of the State of Pennsylvania* (New Haven, 1843), p. 37.
[3]Samuel B. Harding, "Party Struggles over the First Pennsylvania Constitution," *Annual Report* of the American Historical Association, X (1895), 426-59.

the West had long struggled to obtain recognition of its right to fair representation in the Assembly, but there were many who hesitated to reject a charter which they felt had safeguarded public liberties. In spite of the liberalized franchise only six thousand voted. Conservatives made no attempt to name delegates or to vote in the election.[4]

Generally speaking, those who had been active in military organizations or in the local committees of correspondence were the men who were chosen as delegates, not the men of political experience serving in the assembly.[5] The circumstances respecting representation were just the reverse of those which had prevailed during most of the history of the provincial Assembly: the West had twice as many delegates as the East. Thus the convention marks the transfer of power from the people whose ancestors were the original settlers under William Penn to the newer elements in the recently settled regions, together with their political allies, the formerly disfranchised elements in the East.

The convention met on July 15[6] and continued its deliberations until late in September. Benjamin Franklin, just returned from an unsuccessful mission to Montreal undertaken for the purpose of persuading Canada to join the revolutionary movement and heavily burdened with the grave problems being considered by Continental Congress, not only served as a delegate to the convention but also presided over its sessions.[7] Benjamin Frankin, David Rittenhouse (versatile mathematician, astronomer, and radical political spokesman), George Bryan, and James Cannon gave leadership to the radical forces. The radicals were, of course, in control, but a spirited opposition was led by George Clymer and George Ross.[8] In characterizing the convention members one of the conservative opposition charged that not more than one-sixth of the delegates had ever read one word on constitutional subjects!

The constitution adopted was a very liberal one, reflecting as it

---

[4]Joseph A. Nevins, *The American States During and After the Revolution* (New York, 1924), p. 149.

[5]The oath required excluded the Quakers and those unwilling to renounce the King or the government under the Charter. This excluded, of course, the conservative element in the colony. P. L. Ford, "Adoption of the Pennsylvania Constitution of 1776," *Political Science Quarterly*, X (1895), 450.

[6]*The Proceedings Relative to Calling The Conventions of 1776 and 1790* (Harrisburg, 1825), p. 45. The length of the session was in part the consequence of assumption of legislative as well as constituent functions. The convention elected new delegates to Continental Congress. Ford, *op. cit.*, pp. 451-52.

[7]*Proceedings* . . ., 46. Franklin was unanimously chosen president. He was also serving in Continental Congress and had to divide his time between the two assemblies. George Ross was chosen vice president.

[8]Harding, *op. cit.*, p. 376.

did the political views of the frontiersman and of eastern radicals. George Bryan and James Cannon were its chief authors, though Franklin is credited with the provision for a unicameral legislature.[9] It opened with a preamble abjuring allegiance to the British Crown. In its lengthy bill of rights it set forth Whig sentiments similar to those expressed in the Declaration of Independence and those guarantees of personal liberty and of Anglo-Saxon judicial procedures which have since become traditional in American state constitutions.[10] It continued the unicameral legislature that had been established under the Charter of Privileges, and in this single chamber it vested all legislative power.[11] In addition it gave the Assembly authority to select the delegates to Continental Congress,[12] to appoint the state treasurer,[13] and to impeach civil officers.[14] The legislature, it provided, should meet in annual sessions, its members being elected annually.[15] It apportioned representation among the counties on the basis of taxable inhabitants. To avoid the repitition of the injustices under which the West had suffered during the colonial period, it included a provision for periodic reapportionments.[16] In deference to the doctrine of rotation in office, the constitution-makers forbade anyone to serve as a representative for more than four years out of every seven.[17] To insure popular control of legislative action they provided that sessions of the Assembly should be public, legislative proceedings should be published weekly, and all bills should be printed for consideration of the people before third reading. As a further popular check they provided that, except in an emergency,[18] the final passage of every law should be delayed by holding over bills until the assembling of the next session. The reasons or motives for passing laws should be expressed in respective preambles of the bills.

The constitution extended suffrage to all freemen over twenty-one years of age who had paid taxes and had resided in the state for at least a year.[19] It established no religious test for voting, but members of the Assembly were required to declare a belief in one God and in the inspiration of the Scriptures.[20]

The frontier distaste for a strong executive was reflected in the provision substituting an Executive Council for governor. The Executive Council was to be composed of twelve members elected triennially,

---

[9]Ibid.
[10]Ch. I.
[11]Ch. II, Sec. 2.
[12]Ch. II, Sec. 11.
[13]Ch. II, Sec. 9.
[14]Ch. II, Sec. 20.
[15]Ibid.
[16]Ch. II, Sec. 17.
[17]Ch. II, Sec. 8.
[18]Ch. II, Sec. 13, 14, and 15.
[19]Ch. II, Sec. 6.
[20]Ch. II, Sec. 10.

one from each county and the city of Philadelphia. One of its members was to be chosen annually as president of council by a joint vote of the council and the Assembly. In the council the constitution vested the traditional executive powers: appointment of state administrative officers (except the treasurer appointed by the Assembly) and of judges, the enforcement of state laws, and the granting of executive clemency.[21] The council, however, was given none of the legislative powers of the proprietary governor. The legislature, thus, was to operate uninhibited by executive veto. The duties of commander-in-chief of the state militia were vested in the president of council.

The sections dealing with the judiciary provided that courts of justice should be established in the city of Philadelphia and in each county.[22] Courts of session, common pleas and orphans courts were expressly provided for, to be held quarterly in the city and each county, but the Assembly was empowered to create such additional courts as it might deem necessary.[23] Judges of the Supreme Court were to be commissioned for seven years by the Executive Council and were eligible for reappointment; they were made subject to removal at any time by the Assembly for "misbehavior."[24] The justices of the peace, nominated by the freemen and appointed by the president of council, were likewise given seven-year terms.[25] Sheriffs and coroners were to be similarly chosen.[26]

The most curious feature of the constitution of 1776 was the provision for a Council of Censors,[27] elected every seven years (two members from each county and from the city of Philadelphia). The Council of Censors was given the responsibility of inquiring whether or not the officers had performed their duties, and whether any of the provisions of the constitution had been violated. If the council found it absolutely necessary, it might call a convention to consider such amendments as the council deemed necessary. A two-thirds vote in the council was required for such a decision. This was the only provision made for amendment.

After having completed its task the convention unanimously adopted the constitution it had drafted and proclaimed it as the Constitution of Pennsylvania.[28]

---

[21]Ch. II, Sec. 19 and 20.
[22]Ch. II, Sec. 4.
[23]Ch. II, Sec. 26.
[24]Ch. II, Sec. 23.
[25]Ch. II, Sec. 30.
[26]Ch. II, Sec. 31.
[27]Ch. II, Sec. 47.

[28]*Proceedings Relative to the Calling of the Conventions of 1776 and 1790*, p. 54; the convention then committed the new constitution to the keeping of the Council of Safety, *ibid*, p. 66.

The constitution of 1776 was not submitted for popular ratification. Liberals acclaimed it as a remarkable charter of liberty, the product of unselfish devotion to public interest. Eastern conservatives, however, viewed it with misgivings. Late in October protest meetings attended by more than 1,500 were held in Philadelphia.[29] Under the leadership of John Dickinson a series of resolutions were adopted condemning the new constitution and proposing that the government it had created be defeated by failure to elect the officers for which it provided. Petitions were drawn up by the people of Philadelphia and vicinity demanding the calling of a new constitutional convention. Philadelphia even delayed for a time the election of its member on the Executive Council, but finally yielded.[30]

During the difficult period of the Revolutionary War and of postwar reconstruction the constitution of 1776 served as the fundamental charter of the new commonwealth.

---
[29] Harding, *op. cit.*, p. 379.
[30] *Ibid.*, p. 380.

CHAPTER 2: PENNSYLVANIA'S CONSERVATIVE CONSTITUTION OF 1790

JUST as the constitution of 1776 was representative of the political thinking of the radical forces, so the constitution of 1790 reflected the political concepts of the conservatives who regained control in Pennsylvania after the war.

During the Revolutionary War the radical Whigs, called Constitutionalists because of their support of the new constitution, were in control and directed the government vigorously. The Constitutionalists drew their support from the alliance which had framed the constitution, augmented now by most of the Lutheran and Reformed Germans. They were interested in overthrowing the eastern oligarchy as well as in achieving independence from England. They were opposed by the Anti-Constitutionalists including most of the Anglicans, Quakers, non-combatant German sects, and the commercial interests in Philadelphia. With the close of the war, a conservative reaction set in, which finally resulted in the downfall of the Constitutionalists and with them the constitution of which they had served as faithful guardians.[1]

At the close of the war business in Pennsylvania was almost at a standstill. The currency was depreciated until it was almost worthless; many of the former leaders in the economic life of the colony had been Tories and had fled from Philadelphia when British troops were withdrawn; the East had been devastated by the British invasion and the West by Indian ravages. Furthermore, the Constitutionalists at the helm in Pennsylvania, in the main, had been persons inexperienced in political

---

[1] Robert L. Brunhouse, in his carefully documented book *The Counter-Revolution in Pennsylvania, 1776-1790* (Harrisburg, 1942), paints a vivid picture of the politics of the intervening period and demonstrates the degree to which the constitution of 1790 represents a conservative reaction.

affairs. The best leaders of their party were either serving in Congress or in the army. In their zeal for the patriot cause they had adopted many extreme measures which had alienated the less radical forces. With the close of the war their power waned rapidly, and Anti-Constitutionalists (now called Republicans) became outspoken in their demands for constitutional revision. Such was the situation when the time came for the election of the first Council of Censors in 1783.

When the Council met on November 3,[2] its membership was fairly evenly divided between the two factions, and a stormy session ensued. By a close vote the Council declared that the constitution had been violated. A committee was appointed to investigate regarding the defects in the constitution and to suggest remedies.[3] The division of opinion in the Council was reflected in action of the committee, which presented a minority as well as a majority report. The majority report opened with a lengthy criticism of existing institutions, followed by a series of specific proposals. In place of the one-house legislature, on which there was no check save revolution, the revisionists recommended a bicameral legislature restricted by executive veto;[4] instead of the plural executive, which prevented placement of responsibility and rendered decisiveness in emergency difficult, the majority members proposed a single executive.[5] The position assigned to the judiciary, also, was assailed. The seven-year term was too brief and rendered the courts subservient to the will of the executive council which appointed the judges; the power of the Assembly to remove judges at any time for misbehavior made the bench hesitant about declaring laws unconstitutional. Rotation in office was severely censured.[6]

The minority report denounced the action taken by the majority as unconstitutional. It urged the retention without alteration of the existing constitution, which was extolled as the product of harmony and of patriotic fervor, framed in a convention free from factions or mercenary motives, an instrument which had served well in a period of arduous trial.[7]

The majority faction countered with a resolution addressed to the people assailing the minority in vitriolic terms. The calling of a constitutional convention was counseled, but the forces for change were unable to muster the two-thirds vote required by the constitution for the

---

[2]*The Proceedings Relative to the Calling of the Conventions of 1776 and 1790*, p. 67. There was no quorum when it first convened on Nov. 1, *ibid.*, p. 66.
[3]*Ibid.*, p. 68.　　　　　　　　　　[6]*Ibid.*, pp. 66-77.
[4]*Ibid.*, pp. 69, 71.　　　　　　　　[7]*Ibid.*, pp. 77-80.
[5]*Ibid.*, p. 70.

issuance of such a call. On June 1, 1784, the Council adjourned without having taken further action.[8]

A second session of the Council was called for September. Those who favored the existing constitution were now in the majority. An investigation of violations of the constitution was conducted, after which the Council adopted a denunciatory report cataloguing at length alleged transgressions committed by the Assembly. Although petitions were received signed by more than 18,000 persons requesting the calling of a constitutional convention, the Council adjourned on September 25 without having taken favorable action.[9]

Compliance with the provisions of the constitution would have resulted in a delay of at least seven years, with the possibility of a defeat again at the hands of a minority, since a two-thirds vote was necessary. In November, 1789, however, the Assembly, now controlled by the Republicans, assumed extra-constitutional powers and issued the call.[10]

When the convention assembled at Philadelphia on November 24, the conservatives led by James Wilson, Thomas Mifflin, Thomas McKean, and Timothy Pickering, had a majority.[11] The Constitutionalists now abandoned all efforts at obstruction to a fair revision. The document produced was influenced markedly by the federal constitution which had become effective in March of that year.

A governor elected by popular vote for a term of three years was substituted for the plural executive.[12] In him was vested the appointive power,[13] authority to require the opinion in writing of the heads of departments, and the power to grant pardons and reprieves.[14] He was granted a suspensory veto, which could be overruled by a two-thirds vote of both branches of the legislature, and was authorized to call special sessions of the legislature, and to inform that body concerning the state of the commonwealth.[15] The constitution specified that the governor must be at least thirty years of age and a resident of the state for seven years. The governor was made eligible for re-election, but denied the privilege of serving for more than nine years out of any period of twelve years.[16]

Conservative tendencies were further reflected in the abandonment of unicameralism in favor of a two-house legislative body, consist-

---

[8]*Ibid.*, pp. 80-82.
[9]*Ibid.*, pp. 83-128.
[10]*Ibid.*, p. 135. For minutes of the convention see *ibid.*, pp. 137-382.
[11]Brunhouse, *op. cit.*, p. 225.
[14]Art. II, Sec. 9, 10.
[12]Constitution of 1790, Art. II, Sec. 1, 2.
[15]Art. II, Sec. 11, 12.
[13]Art. II, Sec. 8.
[16]Art. II, Sec. 3, 4.

ing of a House of Representatives and a Senate.[17] The House of Representatives, composed of sixty to one-hundred members, apportioned among the counties on the basis of the number of taxable inhabitants (with provision for septennial reapportionment), was to be elected annually. The qualifications prescribed were that members must be at least twenty-one years of age, three years a resident of the state, and a resident for at least one year of the county from which elected.[18] The members of the Senate were given four-year terms, one-fourth of them being elected each year. Age and residence qualifications were set slightly higher than for the House—senators must be at least twenty-five years of age and residents of the state for at least four years. The Senate was assigned eighteen members, but the legislature was authorized to redetermine the number septennially. The total number, however, should never be more than one-third or less than one-fourth the membership of the House.[19] No restrictions were placed on legislative powers, except such as were included in the bill of rights. The power of appointing the state treasurer continued to be vested in the legislature.[20]

Important changes were made in respect to the judiciary. All judges, from justices of the peace to Supreme Court justices, were made appointive by the governor to serve for good behavior.[21] The term of the sheriffs and coroners, who were to be appointed by the governor from the two designated in each case by the local electors, was increased to three years.[22] A new feature was introduced in the provision for division of the state into judicial circuits composed of from three to six counties.[23] The provision for removal of judges by impeachment was retained.[24]

Only a slight modification was made in suffrage qualifications, a two-year residence within the state being substituted for the one-year requirement.[25]

The constitution closed with a statement of the "general, great and essential principles of liberty and free government."[26]

The convention completed its task on February 6, 1790. It then recessed for several months to give the people time to consider the constitution. When the delegates reassembled in September they proclaimed the new document the organic law of the state.

---

[17]Art. I, Sec. 7.
[18]Art. I, Secs. 2, 3, and 4.
[19]Art. I, Secs. 5, 6, 7, and 8.
[20]Art. VI, Sec. 5.
[21]Art. V, Sec. 2.
[22]Art. VI, Sec. 1.
[23]Art. V, Sec. 4.
[24]Art. V, Sc. 10.
[25]Art. III, Sec. 1.
[26]Art. IX.

CHAPTER 3: PENNSYLVANIA'S COMPROMISE CONSTITUTION OF 1838

THE constitution of 1790 was just as truly the product of conservative thinking as the constitution of 1776 had been of radical thinking. It had, therefore, within it the seeds of dissatisfaction once the political pendulum should swing in the other direction. The expression of such dissatisfaction was not long delayed. With the decline of the Federalist party and the rise of Jeffersonian, and later Jacksonian, democracy popular demand for liberalization of the constitution grew. The liberals disapproved of many features of the constitution which they regarded as undemocratic. Believing, as they did, in popular election of officers and limited tenure as the touchstones of democratic polity, they attacked the appointive powers of the governor and demanded popular election of judges and the shortening of the tenure of the governor, senators, and judges. As early as 1805 the Democratic-Republicans waged a vigorous battle for the governorship with constitutional revision as the chief campaign issue. A conservative coalition, rallying to the support of the constitution, succeeded in defeating the revisionists. Three years later, when the Democratic-Republicans captured the governorship with Simon Snyder as their standard bearer, they lost interest in the proposals for curtailment of executive power, but continued to criticize the life-tenure of judges. By 1810 popular petitions for revision flooded the legislature, but the legislature did not respond to this prodding. In 1812 resolutions were introduced in both houses calling for a constitutional convention, but in both instances the resolutions failed. The War of 1812 checked popular interest and agitation.[1]

---

[1]Roy H. Akagi, "The Pennsylvania Constitution of 1838," *The Pennsylvania Magazine*, XLVIII (1924): 301-333, at 303-305.

As is generally true when a popular movement has once been checked, the movement for revision was slow in getting under way again. It was almost a decade before any further action was taken in the legislature, but in the 1820-21 session both the House and the Senate appointed special committees to study the subject. Four years later reform leaders pushed through a resolution providing for the submission to the people of the question of calling a convention. The call was voted down in the referendum that followed, largely because no provision was made for the submission of the proposed convention's work to a subsequent vote of the people. By the time of the 1831-32 session the legislative body was receiving large numbers of popular petitions on the subject. In the 1832-33 session there was a veritable flood of petitions.[2] When the legislature failed to take favorable action a popular "reform convention" was held at Harrisburg, which demanded that the legislature provide for the calling of a convention. In response to this demand the General Assembly in 1835 submitted the issue to popular vote; this time the legislature expressly provided for a subsequent popular referendum on any amendments proposed by the convention.[3] The call was approved by the narrow margin of 13,000 votes. The Democrats supported the proposal, but the Whigs and Antimasons were opposed.[4] The provisions for the election of delegates were enacted at the next session of the legislature.[5]

The Democrats elected sixty-six; the Antimasons, fifty-two; and the Whigs, fifteen delegates. This meant that the Whigs and Antimasons acting as a coalition had a bare majority, but neither side had a "working majority." The result was a compromise, but only after a very lively debate over points of difference.[6]

The convention assembled on May 2, 1837, and continued its deliberations for almost seven months.[7] Included among the distinguished delegates were John Sergeant, Charles Chauncey, William

---

[2]*Ibid.*, pp. 305-310.
[3]1835 Pa. P. L. 151, signed by Governor Wolf April 14, 1835.
[4]The vote was 86,570 for and 73,166 against. The vote went against the call in the following counties: Adams, Bedford, Berks, Bucks, Centre, Chester, Dauphin (close vote), Delaware, Franklin, Juniata, Lancaster (over 7 to 1 against), Lebanon (5 to 1 against); Mifflin, Montgomery (2 to 1 against), Northampton, Northumberland, Perry, Philadelphia, Schuylkill, Somerset (5 to 1 against), Union, and York (14 to 1 against). *Pennsylvania Constitutional Convention, Proceedings and Debates* (1837), preface, p. iv., Vol. I (Cited hereafter as *Proceedings and Debates*.)
[5]1836 Pa. P. L. 70, signed by Governor Wolf March 28, 1836.
[6]Howard M. Jenkins, *Pennsylvania, Colonial and Federal*, II, 280.
[7]Its proceedings filled thirteen volumes.

Meredith, and James Biddle from Philadelphia City; Charles J. Ingersoll from Philadelphia County; Thaddeus Stevens from Adams County; John Dickey and Daniel Agnew from Beaver County; James Porter and James Pollock from Northampton; and George Woodward from Luzerne County. These were the men who took the most active part in debate. John Sergeant, who was elected president of the convention, was "one of the most brilliant and honored men in the legal profession" in Philadelphia, a member of Congress, a candidate for the Vice Presidency with Henry Clay as running mate in 1826, and envoy of the United States to the Panama Congress. Thaddeus Stevens had not yet become known on the national scene, but had won distinction for himself locally by his heroic defense of the public schools in the Pennsylvania Assembly. James Pollock later became governor of the state, and George Woodward later became Chief Justice of the Pennsylvania Supreme Court.[8]

The convention organized by electing its president and other officers, adopted its rules of procedure, and set up nine committees, each to study and prepare a report on one article of the constitution. The legislative procedure of three readings was provided for action in the convention on proposed revisions. By May 16, the convention was organized and ready for business. Already the spirit of controversy that prevailed throughout the long sessions had flared into the open; even the smallest details were debated. Feeling was intensified when, on May 17, Thaddeus Stevens "threw a little firebrand into the convention"[9] by proposing the appointment of a committee on the subject of secret societies and extra-judicial oaths.[10]

The debates of the convention were prolonged and vigorous and marked by an acrimony and exchange of personal abuse which was almost wholly absent in the convention of 1872-73. The convention met in an atmosphere of intense political excitement resulting in part from the hardships of the 1837 panic. The chief issues debated were the governor's powers of appointment, tenure of office, method of choice of judges, the voting franchise, public education, and banking and corporate charters.

During the long period of agitation for revision, one of the primary objects of criticism had been the broad appointive powers of the

---

[8] For the complete list of delegates see *Proceedings and Debates*, I, 10, 11. For description of delegates see Howard M. Jenkins, *op. cit.*, II, 280-1.
[9] Howard M. Jenkins, *op. cit.*, II, 282.
[10] *Debates and Proceedings*, I, 219.

governor, who not only appointed state executive officers, but also all judges and the major county officers as well. It was openly charged that this broad power of patronage had formed the basis for re-election of governors. When, however, the committee on the executive article reported, the majority recommended simply that the governor should have the power to appoint all officers with the advice and consent of the Senate.[11] The constitution of 1790 had not required senatorial approval. Thaddeus Stevens, chairman of the committee, disapproved of this restriction, but believed that the local patronage of the governor should be curtailed. He presented a minority report proposing that prothonotaries, clerks of court, registers of wills, and recorders of deeds should be elective, not appointive.[12] Thomas Bell also prepared a minority report which was presented by the chairman. Bell was opposed to the requirement of senatorial approval for the governor's appointment of the secretary of the commonwealth and the attorney general.[13]

George Woodward of Luzerne County spoke on behalf of the senatorial approval of appointments, insisting that the broader knowledge of appointees by the legislative members would raise the quality of appointments.[14] Thomas Cunningham of Mercer County even urged that approval by the House should be substituted for senatorial approval. This he believed would give the people a greater measure of control over appointments.[15]

The most heated debate arose over the proposals regarding tenure of judges and regulations of banks and other corporations.

The Democrats had long advocated popular election of judges. Since they did not have a majority in the convention, the change from appointment to election had no chance of adoption. Advocates of judicial reform, therefore, centered their attack upon tenure of judges. The majority report of the committee on the judiciary provided for appointment of judges for life tenure on good behavior.[16] George Woodward of Luzerne County presented a minority report proposing a ten-year term for Supreme Court judges, a seven-year term for common pleas judges, and a five-year term for associate common pleas judges.[17] When the report came up on first reading in Committee of the Whole, he moved the substitution of the minority provision. This ushered in a long debate. Joseph Hopkinson of Philadelphia delivered the chief address against the proposed change. In an eloquent and

---

[11]*Ibid.*, I, 534.
[12]*Ibid.*, p. 534-535.
[13]*Ibid.*, p. 535.
[14]*Ibid.*, II, 288, 289. Cunningham was speaker of the state Senate.
[15]*Ibid.*, II, 325-328.
[16]*Ibid.*, I, 357.
[17]*Ibid.*, pp. 357-8.

learned address of considerable length he defended the principle of judicial independence as essential to justice. He pointed to the irregularities that had existed under the 1776 constitution, when the judges were denied the independence springing from unlimited tenure.[18] To this Woodward replied at length, reviewing the history of judicial tenure in English and Pennsylvania courts. Life-tenancy, he insisted, was not essential for independence. The reduction in tenure proposed in the amendment was essential "to make the judges in some degree accountable to the people." He pointed to the fact that in the petitions to the legislature during the preceding decade reform of judicial tenure had been the chief concern.[19]

There were demands, also, for popular election of judges, but the coalition majority made it impossible to put through this reform.

Woodward was joined by Charles Brown of Philadelphia County, John Sergeant and Charles Chauncey of Philadelphia City, and John Dickey of Beaver County in his fight for reform. James M. Porter of Northampton and George Chambers of Franklin supported Hopkinson's position. After much discussion, John Dickey proposed a compromise, providing for a fifteen-year term for Supreme Court judges, and ten and five years, respectively, for president and associate judges in common pleas courts. This amendment was accepted in Committee of the Whole[20] and later approved by the convention.[21]

Debates over the suffrage provisions extended for more than a week, with sharp division of opinion over property qualifications, residential and taxpaying requirements, and racial qualifications.[22] The western Democrats urged the sweeping aside of taxpaying qualifications. In reply to those who insisted that only persons who owned property and paid taxes should have the right to control the property of others, H. G. Rogers of Allegheny County asked, "does property, merely, elevate the character of an individual?—does it brighten the intellectual vision or fit the possessor in any degree, for the better discharge of the duties of a citizen?" Expressing the viewpoint of the West, he declared, "If in my power, I would found this government

---

[18] *Ibid.*, IV, 278-315; for Woodward's motion to amend, see IV, 277.
[19] *Ibid.*, IV, 315-345. These two speeches attest to the hardihood of the delegates. Together they cover 67 pages! The quotation from Woodward's speech appears on p. 345.
[20] *Ibid.*, IV, 378-9 for Dickey's proposal; V, 138, for adoption of the amendment. The vote was 60 to 48.
[21] *Ibid.*, X, 255.
[22] Debate lasted from June 19 to June 28, *Ibid.*, II, 470 to III, 178.

upon two broad and enduring pillars—universal suffrage and general education."[23] Conservative forces in the convention, however, were strong enough to prevent the removal of the taxpaying qualification.

There was also a verbal skirmish over the length of the residence qualification and an unsuccessful attempt to prevent the restriction of voting to "white" male citizens. Phineas Jenks of Bucks County opposed the insertion of the word "white," which had not appeared in the 1790 constitution. Jenks pointed out that there were Negroes in Bucks County with property worth $20,000 to $100,000, and said he did not see why they should be barred from voting.[24] Thomas Earle and Charles Chauncey of Philadelphia supported the proposal,[25] but Benjamin Martin and William Meredith, also of Philadelphia, opposed it. Martin declared that if the convention attempted to give Negroes the right to vote, it would be attempting more than it could carry out. "Any attempt to amend the Constitution to place the black population on an equal footing with the white population," he asserted, "would prove ruinous to the black people." Any attempt on their part to exercise the suffrage in Philadelphia County would certainly "bring ruin upon their own heads." Public sentiment would rise above the law. It would be unwise to hold out to the Negroes expectations which could not be realized.[26]

The proposal was defeated by a vote of 77 to 45,[27] and "white" was incorporated into the voting qualifications.

Over a month was devoted to the discussion of banking and general corporation issues, and by far the bitterest exchanges between delegates came over this issue. The majority of the special committee dealing with this subject reported that it was "unnecessary and inexpedient" to make any changes in the constitution on these subjects.[28]

---

[23]*Ibid.*, II, 474-5.
[24]*Ibid.*, II, 476.
[25]Earle, who opposed voting strictures, whether based on race or property ownership, declared that he would "permit them [the poor] to employ all the rights of men, and if they abuse those rights, the rich will perhaps set about improving their character and condition by education and wholesome laws. He would give every man a vote because he was a man, and because if you do not give him a vote he is governed by laws which he has no voice in making. He would give every man a voice in the choice of his masters, so that if he is oppressed by them he could have the opportunity of changing them. . . . This was the true principle of democracy, and he wished to have it carried out in our elections . . ." *Ibid.*, II, 554-557.
[26]*Ibid.*, II, 477.
[27]*Ibid.*, X, 106.
[28]Report of the Committee on Currency, Corporations, Public Highways and Eminent Domain, *ibid.*, I, 358. Debate in Committee of the Whole extended from

There was a strong opposition, however, led by C. J. Ingersoll of Philadelphia County, who presented the minority report. In terms which many delegates regarded as inflammatory, he denounced the banks for their suspension of payment of their notes and for the part they had played in the speculation that had precipitated the panic which then held not only Pennsylvania, but the whole country in its throttling grasp.[29] "The whole theory and practice of American banks," he declared, "are false and pernicious; their first act being to lend trust money, left for them to keep; their next misconduct is to issue mere promissory notes, instead of gold and silver.... They then make loans of fictitious credit, by secret and arbitrary discounts, increased or decreased with no regard for public good."[30] He demanded more stringent regulation of the issuance of bank charters and strict supervision of the note issues by banks. He referred to the commercial classes as "those indulged favorites of the American Government, for whom navies, foreign wars and large expenditures" had been made at the expense of the agricultural and mechanical classes. He referred also to the costly encouragement by the government of manufacturing. This protection, he granted was legitimate, since the prosperity of every class was essential for the common welfare; but, he added, "no class has a right to supremacy, much less has any individual, or a few, the least right to privileges at the expense of the rest of the community."[31] In order to correct existing evils, he proposed that charters without time limitations or authorizing monopolies for private purposes should be prohibited and, as a further protection for public interest, that charters should be granted by a two-thirds vote in two successive sessions of the legislature.

November 29 to December 29; the debates are recorded from page 36 of volume 6 to volume 8, page 86.

[29]The report read in part: "The shocking vicissitudes of an unconvertible paper medium are but too familiar to all experience. They have cost this country more than all its wars. They were the greatest difficulty of the Revolution; and they are at this moment, the most oppressive, by far, of all public burthens. They have caused a calamitous convulsion.... No law can create capital at a stroke. It is the slow growing offspring of industry and liberty alone... Preposterous luxury, insolvency and crime are certain followers of the bank mania, a system of stupendous gambling supersedes and derides regular occupations . . . With eighty millions of gold and silver and abundance of everything needful for prosperity and content, large portions of our people are in a revolutionary state of disquiet and excitement, are reduced to want, and maddened with disappointment." *Ibid.*, I, 358-367 William Brown, C. Myers and Mark Darragh also signed the minority report.

[30]*Ibid.*, VI, 363.

[31]*Ibid.*, VI, 362.

To this assault upon the banks Thaddeus Stevens replied in bitter terms of denunciation, urging the convention to refrain from publishing the report. With characteristic vehemence he declared that he had "never listened to anything so incendiary in its principles and absurd in its arguments as this most extraordinary document." He then went on to ask whether at "a time when the whole community was ready for an explosion; when a magazine was laid which a single spark would cause to explode to the disaster and utter ruin of the whole community" the convention would permit a member of that body "to lay the train and apply the torch?"[32]

After further verbal skirmish the convention voted 68 to 57 to print the report.[33] The bitterness displayed foreshadowed the fight that would be provoked by this subject when it was reached on first reading in Committee of the Whole. As soon as the majority report had been read an amendment was moved by Almon H. Read of Susquehanna proposing that stockholders should be liable for the debts of corporations. This was defeated by the convention.[34] He then proposed an amendment prohibiting banks from issuing notes of less denomination than $20.[35] These proposals reflected the point of view of the Jacksonian Democrats. Thaddeus Stevens then introduced a substitute amendment which simply stated: "The Legislature shall provide wholesome restrictions on all banking institutions within this Commonwealth, so as to promote the best interests of all the people."[36] This opened up the discussion of the entire subject of banking, currency, and corporations. Debate was conducted with a vigor and asperity which not only ruffled dispositions of opposing delegates, but must have shaken the rafters.

James Clarke of Indiana County launched a bitter attack upon banks and other corporate interests, castigating them as creators of an artificial aristocracy of wealth.[37] Charles Chauncey[38] and George Chambers of Franklin County[39] joined Thaddeus Stevens in a vigorous defense of the Whig position on banks and corporations. Stevens insisted that neither the banks nor corporations were the culprits in the existing economic crisis. He blamed the collapse of the economy upon President Jackson and his Specie Circular.[40]

---

[32]*Ibid.*, I, 368-9.
[33]*Ibid.*, I, 391.
[34]*Ibid.*, V, 468.
[35]*Ibid.*, VI, 34.
[36]*Ibid.*, VI, 36.

[37]*Ibid.*, VI, 80-86; 88-95.
[38]*Ibid.*, VII, 411-429.
[39]*Ibid.*, VIII, 24-34.
[40]*Ibid.*, VII, 132-137; 154-167.

After exhaustive examination of the issue the convention, finally, on December 29, adopted a resolution stating, as the majority report had recommended, that it was inexpedient to make any changes in Art. VII, Sec. 3 of the constitution.[41]

Another subject of lively discussion was the provision respecting public education. This was not surprising considering the fact that the convention met so soon after the bitter fight in the contest for governor fought on the issue of repeal of the public school law of 1834. Thaddeus Stevens' valiant defense that saved the free schools in the 1835 legislative session was fresh in the minds of all. Opponents of free schools were not yet reconciled. When the committee on education proposed that provision should be made for the education of children of the poor at public expense,[42] Thaddeus Stevens took the floor to demand that the provision "be broadened to include all children without inquiry into wealth or poverty." There "should be no legal paupers," he thundered, "and no dividing distinction of this kind should be incorporated into an organic law."[43] Stevens, however, did not succeed in changing majority sentiment, and the provision of the old constitution was carried over into the new.[44]

The first reading was completed by December 29 after eight months of stormy debate; the second reading was completed by February 7, though the vigor of debate indicated that tempers had not cooled. Two weeks later the third reading was completed and the task of the constitution-makers was finished.

The main structure of the government as it had been set up under the constitution of 1790 remained unchanged under the new document. "Supreme executive power" remained in the hands of the governor.[45] The governor's appointive powers were, however, curtailed; many officers previously appointed by him were made elective.[46] The gover-

---

[41]Approved in Committee of the Whole by vote of 64-54, *ibid.*, VIII, 88. On Dec. 19, Almon Read had withdrawn his original amendment, and Steven's amendment to the amendment fell with it; Read then proposed a new amendment forbidding any bank which was chartered, rechartered or revived in the future to issue bills or promissory notes of less than ten dollars, *ibid.*, VII, 224. This was rejected on Dec. 29, following which the proposal of the majority report was adopted.

[42]*Ibid.*, V, 183.

[43]*Ibid.*, V, 300.

[44]Constitution of 1790, Art. VII, Sec. 1, "The legislature shall, as soon as conveniently may be, provide by law for the establishment of schools throughout the State, in such manner that the poor may be taught gratis."

[45]Art. II, Sec. 1.

[46]Prothonotaries, clerks of court, registers of wills, recorders of deeds were made

nor's term of office remained three years, but he could not serve more than six years out of any period of nine years.[47] The secretary of the commonwealth, created by the constitution of 1790, was continued on an appointive basis.[48] The treasurer remained elective by the legislature.[49]

New limitations were imposed upon legislative authority. The legislature was forbidden to grant divorces by legislative act.[50] It was also forbidden to create, renew, or extend bank charters without six months public notice. It could not grant private corporate charters of any kind running for more than twenty years. A separate act was required for each corporation when charters were granted or renewed.[51] In order to limit the effects of the United States Supreme Court in *Dartmouth College v. Woodward* it was further provided that the legislature should have the right to alter, revoke, or amend any charter it might subsequently grant.[52] The legislature was forbidden to delegate the power of eminent domain to any private corporation unless it required such corporation to pay for the private property taken.[53] This was the beginning of the movement for the restriction of the substantive powers of the state legislature, which reached its peak at the time of the meeting of the 1872-73 constitutional convention.

The judiciary, the chief target of liberal attacks, was subjected to considerable overhauling. The provisions for life tenure were removed from the organic law. Supreme Court judges were given fifteen-year terms; the president judge of the county common pleas court, a ten-year term; and associate common pleas judges, a five-year term.[54] The governor retained the power to appoint these judges, with the advice and consent of the Senate.[55] Justices of the peace, sheriffs, and coroners henceforth were to be elected. The justice of the peace was given a five-year term and the two peace officers a three-year term.[56] The circuit courts of the 1790 constitution were abandoned.

Suffrage qualifications were subjected to slight modification. The length of residence in the state was reduced to one year, but a ten-day

---

elective (except prothonotaries of the Supreme Court, which were to be appointed by the court itself). Art. VI, Sec. 6. Sheriffs, coroners, justices of the peace and aldermen also were made elective. Art. VI, Secs. 1 and 7.

[47] Art. II, Sec. 3.
[48] Art. II, Sec. 8.
[49] Art. II, Sec. 6.
[50] Art. I, Sec. 14.
[51] Art. I, Sec. 25.

[52] Art. I, Sec. 26.
[53] Art. VII, Sec. 4.
[54] Art. V, Sec. 2.
[55] Art. V, Sec. 2.
[56] Art. VI, Sec. 7.

residence period in the voting district was added. The taxpaying requirement was retained. For the first time the constitution expressly limited voting to "white" persons.[57]

The new constitution introduced provision for amendment. The provision established a procedure identical with that now in force. The proposed amendment must be approved by a majority vote of the whole number of members in each house in two successive sessions. Provision was made for publicity by advertisement. Proposed amendments could be ratified by a majority vote of those voting on the amendment in a popular referendum. No amendments could be submitted to the people more often than once in five years.[58]

When the new constitution was submitted for popular approval it was ratified, but only by a very close vote—113,971 to 112,759.[59] The chief support came from the northern and western counties and the chief opposition from the German counties and the large cities.[60] During the period of debate preceding the referendum, officeholders, particularly judges, whose tenure was impaired by the new constitution, not only opposed the ratification "with a very general unanimity," but with "intense and aggressive hostility."[61] Generally speaking, Whigs and Antimasons more often clung to the "matchless instrument" of 1790 and Democrats more often embraced the new constitution, but the voting lines were not clearly drawn on a party basis.[62]

The conservative majority in the convention had prevented a revision on the thoroughgoing basis desired by the Jacksonian Democrats and thus forced a compromise, but this is not to say that the new fundamental law introduced no significant change. Alexander K. McClure in his *Old Time Notes of Pennsylvania* says of the constitution that the "vital feature" was the "resumption of power by the people in taking from the Executive nearly all his patronage, and making most offices elective."[63]

The constitution of 1838 remained the basic charter until January 1, 1874. During its thirty-six years of operation it was amended on four occasions. In 1850, the advocates of popular election of judges finally

---

[57] Art. III, Sec. 1.
[58] Art. X.
[59] *Proceedings and Debates*, XIII, 260-261.
[60] Isaac Sharpless, *op. cit.*, 309-310.
[61] Alexander K. McClure *Old Time Notes of Pennsylvania*, I, 39.
[62] *Ibid.*, I, 71-72.
[63] I, 72.

won out. By constitutional amendment all judges were made elective.[64] Thus ended successfully a half century of agitation.[65]

Again in 1857 the constitution was amended. The number of representatives in the General Assembly was set at one hundred, elected from separate districts. The remainder of the amendments adopted at that time placed various restrictions upon state legislative power. Most significant were the limitations upon borrowing power and upon the power to create new counties.[66] The limitations on borrowing power were a consequence of the recent unhappy experience in the handling of the indebtedness incurred in the construction of the internal improvements generally called the Great Works Project and the political repercussions from the sale of portions of the project to private railroad corporations at a fraction of original cost. Abuses of land developers in promoting legislation for the creation of new counties was responsible for the limitation regarding the creation of new counties.

In 1864 the right of absentee voting was extended to soldiers absent from their regular voting districts in military service.[67] At the same time two new strictures were imposed upon the legislature. That body was forbidden to pass any bill other than an appropriation bill containing more than one subject. It was further provided that each bill should contain a title clearly expressing the purpose of the bill.[68] The legislature was also forbidden to pass any legislation granting powers or privileges which it was within the power of the courts to confer.[69]

The final amendment came in 1871, on the very eve of the calling

---

[64] Amendment to Art. V, Sec. 2.

[65] McClure says that the success of the movement was hastened by the intemperate attacks of judges upon the Constitution of 1838, and by the political trickery used by some incumbent judges to extend their terms. *Ibid.*, I, 39. ff.

[66] Art. 1, Sec. 4 originally gave the legislature the power to set the number of representatives (not less than sixty or more than one hundred); the Amendment of 1857 established the number at one hundred. Two new articles were added. Art. XI limited borrowing power, stating the purposes for which the state could borrow, limiting the debt for "casual deficiencies in revenue" to $750,000, and requiring the establishment of a sinking fund to pay off the debt. The legislature was forbidden to pledge or loan the credit of the commonwealth to any individual, company or corporation, or to make the commonwealth a stockholder or owner of a private company or corporation. Art. XII forbade the dividing of a county in such a way as to deprive it of more than one-tenth of its population without the assent of the electors of that county, or create a new county containing less than four hundred square miles.

[67] This amendment became Sec. 4 of Art. III.

[68] Art. XI, Sec. 8.

[69] Art. XI, Sec. 9.

of the next constitutional convention. At this time the state treasurer was made elective.[70]

---

[70]Art. VI, Sec. 6. This was not simply a climax to the Jacksonian movement for popular election of administrative officials. It was the consequence of the scandals surrounding the election of the state treasurer in 1869, when there were public charges of legislative corruption.

PART TWO

Pennsylvania's Reform Constitution of 1874

CHAPTER *4:* ECONOMIC, SOCIAL, AND POLITICAL SETTING, 1874

In four great provinces bound together by ever-constricting ties of federation—manufacturing, extractive industries, transportation and finance—the leaders of business enterprise, sustained and assisted by a host of liegemen, marched from victory to victory in the decades that followed the triumph of Grant at Appomattox.

CHARLES BEARD[1]

THE Pennsylvania constitution of 1874 is the longest and the most detailed of the four fundamental documents under which the commonwealth has been governed. It was drafted in an atmosphere of extreme distrust of the legislative body and of fear of the growing power of corporations, especially of the great railroad corporations. It was the product of a convention whose prevailing mood was one of reform—reform of the election process to prevent fraud and stealing of elections; reform of social evils in a variety of categories; reform of the practices of railroads and other corporations and curtailment of their powers; and, overshadowing all else, reform of legislation to eliminate the evil practices that had crept into the legislative process. Legislative reform was truly the dominant motif of the convention and that purpose is woven into the very fabric of the constitution. Some members of the convention did seem vaguely to sense that the commonwealth was on the threshold of a new era, which would usher in new social and economic problems. The convention was, nevertheless, more concerned with setting up safeguards to prevent the repetition of past abuses than with the creative

---

[1]*The Rise of American Civilization,* II, 176.

task of building a fundamental charter adequate for the needs of the future.

The period following the Civil War had been a period of a rapidly expanding economy in Pennsylvania as well as in many other states, and this expanding economy was reflected in corporate development. It had also been an era in which political morality was at a low ebb. Under the then existing system, charters of business corporations and of municipal corporations as well were granted by special law. A separate legislative act was necessary to create each new corporation; franchises for railroads and other utilities were similarly granted. Local governments were completely at the mercy of the legislative body. State legislatures in the face of the tremendous pressures of the time had often sacrificed public interests to private or personal interests; charges of abuse of trust were widespread.

The Civil War gave a strong impetus to extractive industries and manufactures in the United States, and these interests continued to grow in the postwar years. This growth was matched with expanding railroad transportation (financed in large part by foreign capital) and growth of finance. Pennsylvania stood in the front ranks in economic growth, prospering in manufacturing, mining, transportation, banking, and trade. The period following the Civil War was, certainly, one of singular prosperity for all phases of the economy of Pennsylvania, though portions of the state had not escaped the ravages of war.[2]

Real and personal property values in Pennsylvania rose spectacularly during the decades from 1850 to 1870. The combined property values increased from $722,500,000 in 1850 to $1,500,000,000 in 1860, and more than doubled during the next decade, reaching $3,750,000,000 by 1870.[3] During the same period the United States as a whole experienced a growth in such property values of from $7,250,000,000 in 1850 to $16,250,000,000 in 1860, and an increase from that level to $32,000,000,000 in 1870.[4] Pennsylvania, thus, outpaced the nation in the growth of property values during the decade from 1860 to 1870. Its property values in 1870 represented one-eighth of the total property holdings in the entire country.

Pennsylvania was also in the front ranks in the growth of general manufactures. By 1850, Pennsylvania ranked third in value of manu-

---

[2] In Adams, Bedford, Cumberland, Franklin, and York counties there was "much suffering and hardship" as a consequence of such ravages. Francis A. Godcharles, *Pennsylvania, Political, Governmental, Military and Civil*, I, 330.

[3] *Ninth Census*, 1870, III, 11 (All figures are given in round numbers).

[4] *Ibid.*

factures produced, being exceeded only by New York and Massachusetts. In the decade between 1850 and 1860, the value of output almost doubled, but Pennsylvania remained third in rank.[5] Manufacturing was highly diversified in character.[6]

The next decade was one of marked growth: capital investments in manufactures rose to $407,000,000 by 1870. Output in that year was valued at $712,000,000, and Pennsylvania rose to second place in the value of output. Only New York outdistanced it in output, number of persons employed, and wages paid by manufactures; and Pennsylvania outranked even New York in the number of establishments and capital investment.[7]

Heavy industry also expanded at a rapid pace. Pennsylvania was the leading producer of steel and iron products. Steel producing establishments in the state increased from five in 1850 to nine in 1860, at a time when there were but thirteen such establishments in the entire country. Pennsylvania was then producing more than half of the national output.[8] Pressures of the war and postwar prosperity increased the number of establishments in Pennsylvania to eighteen by 1870.[9] Capital investment which had stood at but $52,300,000 in 1850 had risen to $1,345,000,000 in 1860, and reached the four billion mark by 1870. The increase in value of production rose even more spectacularly during the last mentioned decade. While capital investment tripled, output rose from $1,330,000,000 to approximately $7,000,000,000.[10] In the manufacture of iron and steel products Pennsylvania also was dominant. In 1870 there were over a thousand establishments engaged in such production, and Pennsylvania could claim credit for almost half of all the

---

[5]*Ibid.*, III, 562.

[6]Wayland F. Dunaway, *Pennsylvania History*, pp. 648, 653; 664-667. Pennsylvania was an important producer of cotton goods and clothing; woolens and worsted goods; hosiery and knit goods; carpets and rugs; leather and leather products, including women's and children's clothes, lumber and furniture. It ranked second only to New York in shipbuilding and ranked first in the cigar industry. It produced one-fourth of all malt beverages in the United States.

[7]*Ninth Census Report*, III, 562. There were 37,200 establishments employing 320,000 persons, who received $125,000,000 in wages in 1870. 222,000 steam horsepower and 142,000 horsepower produced by water wheels were also employed.

[8]*Ibid.*, III, 675.

[9]*Ibid.* During the same period steam horsepower used in steel production rose from 40 in 1850, to 592 in 1860, to a spectacular 8,917 by 1870. By contrast steam horsepower similarly employed in England was only 1,813 in 1870.

[10]*Ibid.*

iron products manufactured in the United States.[11] The production of fencing, nails, wire and wire products, spikes, railings, and wrought-iron pipes had become an important branch of the steel and iron industry.[12] By 1872 there were 276 blast furnaces distributed over the coal and iron counties, and about a dozen more under construction.

In the manufacture of railway rails Pennsylvania made a significant contribution. By 1872 Pennsylvania was producing 420,000 tons of such rails, about 44½ per cent of all rail products in the United States.[13]

The extractive industries, too, were in a vigorous stage of growth during the 1860-70 decade. The Pennsylvania petroleum industry, representing an investment of nine and a quarter million dollars, dominated that industry. In 1870, Pennsylvania production reached the $18,000,000 mark, at a time when its nearest rival, West Virginia, produced but $1,000,000 worth of petroleum products.[14] The Pennsylvania coal industry also felt the impetus of the era of expansion. Anthracite production jumped from nine and a half million tons in 1860 to over fourteen million by 1870.[15] Bituminous coal production also rose; the total produced by Pennsylvania mines in 1870 was almost eight million tons. The coal mining industry represented capital investment of $68,000,000. The combined anthracite and bituminous production of 1870 was valued at $52,300,000; Pennsylvania ranked first both in tonnage produced and in value of output. By contrast, Illinois, the next highest producer, mined only $6,000,000 worth of coal.[16]

---

[11]136 out of a total for the U. S. of 386 establishments producing pig iron were in Pennsylvania. In 1870 Pennsylvania produced 1,189,000 tons of pig iron out of a total U. S. production of 2,388,000 tons. There were 524 establishments located in Pennsylvania engaged in the production of cast iron and 274 in production of forged and rolled iron. "Pennsylvania in its Industrial Aspects," *Republic*, 2:261-8 (1874) at p. 267.

[12]Wayland F. Dunaway, *op. cit.*, p. 653; *Republic*, 2 (1874); 264-5.

[13]"Pennsylvania in its Industrial Aspects," *loc. cit.*, p. 265. This was exclusive of 15,000 tons of street railway rails and mining rails. The total output for the U. S. in that year was 530,800; the U. S. imported 530,850 tons (a decline of 6½ per cent from the preceding year).

[14]*Ninth Census*, III, Table XIV, 769. Two years later the *Pittsburgh Gazette*, Aug. 27, 1872, reported the "coming in" of the "Largest Well Now Known" at Butler, Pa., with 400 bbls. a day flow of oil. In 1873 almost 2,000,000 bbls. of oil were exported from the port of Philadelphia; total foreign exports from the United States in that year stood at 5,742,000. Pennsylvania exports, thus, equalled one-third of our foreign export of that commodity. "Pennsylvania in its Industrial Aspects," *loc. cit.*, p. 264. By 1873 the largest well in Pennsylvania was producing 1,000 bbls. a day.

[15]*Ninth Census*, III, 767; *Annual Report*, Anthracite Division, Department of Mines (Pennsylvania), 1949, p. 4.

[16]*Ninth Census*, III, Table XIV, 767.

The extraction of iron ore also was important in Pennsylvania economy. With $4,500,000 capital investment, the ore industry in 1870 produced an output valued at $4,000,000.[17]

Business activity was reflected in the growth of banking and insurance. In 1873 there were 204[18] banks with assets totaling $218.6 million.[19] Capital stock had grown to $53 million; surplus, to $17.5 million; and undivided profits, to $2 million. Individual deposits totaled $84.8 million, half of that amount in Philadelphia banks.[20]

The Commissioner of Industrial Statistics pointed with pride to the volume of Pennsylvania insurance premiums. By 1870, fire and marine insurance premiums paid by Pennsylvanians to Pennsylvania and out of state companies had reached $15.6 million, and life insurance premiums totaled $8 million more, bringing the grand total to $23.6 million. This he explained was equal to $6.30 per capita, and three times the entire revenue of the state government![21]

This tremendous economic development was reflected also in the growth of the corporate structure of business. Since charters were granted by special acts of the legislature, the legislators were subjected to strong pressures. Most of the legislation enacted during this period consisted of special legislation, much of it in the form of grants of corporate power, authorization of increased capitalization, authorization of increased borrowing, and similar measures. So great was the legislative activity in this area that scant attention was given to general legislation.[22] A leading Republican newspaper stated that a majority of the members of the legislature considered time spent on anything but private bills as a waste of time.[23] The same journal, editorializing on the

---

[17]*Ibid.*, p. 768.

[18]There were 29 in Philadelphia; 16 in Pittsburgh; and 159 in the rest of the state. *Second Annual Report*, Pennsylvania Bureau of Industrial Statistics (1873-74), p. 74.

[19]Assets of Philadelphia banks slightly exceeded $90.8 million; Pittsburgh banks, $32.9; and the remaining banks, $94.8 million, *loc. cit.*

[20]*Loc. cit.*

[21]*Loc. cit.*, p. 62.

[22]Of the 1872 session pamphlet laws, 1,145 acts covering 1,493 pages were special acts; only 48, covering 75 pages, were general laws. (Special acts also included acts dealing with municipal corporations as well as private corporations, and with individuals, but the majority dealt with business corporations.) In 1870 the pamphlet laws ran about 2,000 pages and in 1871, about 1,700 pages; the proportion of public and private bills ran approximately the same as for 1872. Statistics taken from editorial in the *Pittsburgh Gazette*, October 21, 1872.

[23]*Pittsburgh Gazette*, March 6, 1873. The editor cited the case of the local option bill, which, in spite of strong popular demand, was delayed and almost defeated "because it infringed on the time the members desired for their private schemes."

evils of special legislation, stated that it had given birth "to a brood of brokers and speculators in the law, which have become the parents of legislative bribery and corruption." Such "brokers" obtained the passage of laws granting charters of incorporation loosely drawn, with purposes hidden in vague terms, granting broad powers with few limitations. Such charters could be adapted to any scheme desired.[24] They were then "hawked about major cities" and sold to the highest bidder. Such, allegedly, was the origin of the charter used for the notorious Credit Mobilier scheme.[25] Anticipating demand for particular types of charters, lobbyists not uncommonly put through the charters, then offered them for sale to the interested parties. Since it was often cheaper for the charter applicant to purchase the charter from a lobbyist than to push it through the legislative gauntlet, lobbyists were able to collect their "blackmail."[26] The legislature at times helped these hucksters of "floating" charters by refusing to enact charters for persons wishing to incorporate so that they would have to purchase at enhanced prices charters already authorized.[27] Bills hostile to corporate interests were also introduced and used as weapons to force payment of tribute as the price for their defeat. Indeed, it was charged that when charters were acted on favorably at Harrisburg, a graduated tariff was assessed for the passage of the bills, the rate charged depending upon "the degree to which 'a good thing' is seen to lurk in the charter."[28] This price, as indicated, often exceeded the price charged on the open market.

Senator A. K. McClure of Philadelphia, who had served in the state legislature for sixteen years,[29] said of this period, "venality in legisla-

---

[24]*Pittsburgh Gazette*, Oct 21, 1872. The editor cited the case of the South Improvement Company which was used in an attempt to monopolize the petroleum industry.

[25]See statement of H. G. Smith, delegate to the Constitutional Convention, *Debates of the Constitutional Convention*, 1872-1873, I, 420. He stated that the charter used was passed in skeleton form conferring the "most ample powers, and capable of being applied to almost any corporate purpose." The passage of skeleton charters with the most liberal grants of corporate powers was a common practice. "They are articles of merchandise, and you can go to certain parties in this city [Philadelphia] and elsewhere and buy a charter under which almost any conceivable business may be carried on." Their price in the past had been very cheap, but the calling of the convention, he stated, had run up the rate.

[26]*Pittsburgh Gazette*, Oct. 22, 1872. The editor cited, as a case in point, the fact that a notorious lobbyist had put through the 1871 session a bank charter (anticipating demand for such a charter in Philadelphia). When the Philadelphia bankers would not take the charter at the handsome sum he asked, he had the charter amended to extend to Pittsburgh. He then sold it for $5,000 in Pittsburgh.

[27]Silas Clark (of Indiana County) speaking at the Convention, *Debates*, IV, 587.

[28]*Pittsburgh Gazette*, Oct. 21, 1872.

[29]From 1858-1874.

tion reached its tidal wave."[30] It invaded every phase of the legislative process. The enactment of charter legislation and of other private bills was facilitated by logrolling. Many bills were passed which could not possibly have been put through on the basis of their merits, but combinations of special interests supporting each other's bills were able to force them through. Bank charters were generally put through in blocks of a dozen or more, and support for these was traded off for support of other private bills. Under these circumstances the lobbyist became the key man in legislation. There were, McClure stated "a dozen men who amassed liberal fortunes by plying their vocations as lobbyists. They were men of unusual intelligence and sagacity, some of whom held important political positions." Although there were serving in the legislature "men of purest purpose and sternest integrity," it was nevertheless true that by seeing the leaders in the two houses, arrangement could be made and the desired number of votes delivered for suitable compensation.[31]

For railroads in Pennsylvania this same decade was an important era of development and consolidation and of power in Pennsylvania politics. Taylor and Neu,[32] commenting on Pennsylvania railroads at the beginning of the decade, state that they fell generally into two divisions:

(1) those in the eastern part of the state, north and northwest of Philadelphia, which were for the most part anthracite roads; and (2) those that led westward and were designed to give Philadelphia control of the trade of Susquehanna Valley and western Pennsylvania, as well as to provide, via Pittsburgh, an avenue of commerce with the Ohio Valley.

The development of the eastern lines, of which the Philadelphia and Reading Railroad was the most important, was dominated by the interests of investors in anthracite coal lands and of Philadelphia commercial interests competing with New York City. So strong was the rivalry between the two cities that Pennsylvania lines were deliberately isolated from those of adjoining states. Philadelphia, indeed, was "a major obstacle to the through movement of passengers and freight." Though there were lines leading to New York and to Baltimore which entered Pennsylvania and extended to or near the city, they were not permitted to connect their lines in Philadelphia. All goods had to be carried from

---

[30] A. K. McClure, *Old Time Notes of Pennsylvania*, II, 412.

[31] *Ibid.*, pp. 410-421.

[32] George R. Taylor and Irene D. Neu, *The American Railroad Networks*, Harvard University Press, 1956, p. 26.

one railroad line to the other by dray, and passengers, by inadequate railway service, on horse drawn cars! Only by a threat that Congress, in order to meet Civil War needs, would authorize a federally subsidized line from Washington to New York, were Philadelphia interests induced to yield in 1863 and permit railroad connections.[33]

Rivalry between Philadelphia and Baltimore commercial interests gave birth to the Pennsylvania Railroad. In 1842, the Baltimore & Ohio Railroad, which had completed a line to Cumberland, Maryland, sought from the Pennsylvania legislature a franchise that would authorize it to extend its line to Pittsburgh. Pittsburgh, at this time, was connected with Philadelphia by the Great Works Project, that curious combination of canals, mountain portages, and railways (horse drawn in the early days) which was a marvel in its day. A steam railroad line would, however, render this system obsolete, and Philadelphia merchants were shocked into action by this attempt to divert western trade from their city to a rival entrepôt of trade.[34] They wrung from the legislature an act providing that if a new company was organized with $3,000,000

---

[33]*Ibid.*, p. 28. Philadelphia interests in 1852 had pushed through the legislature a measure prohibiting the laying of broad-gauge lines, except in a designated area near the Ohio border. This was designed to prevent further extension of the two major New York lines that had entered Pennsylvania, the Delaware, Lackawanna and Western R.R. which connected the coal country of northeastern Pennsylvania with New York and the Erie R.R. which at two points dipped into northern Pennsylvania. *Ibid.*, pp. 26-27.

[34]William B. Wilson, in his monumental *History of the Pennsylvania Railroad Company* describes the struggle in vivid terms:

When the Seventieth Session of the Legislature of the Commonwealth of Pennsylvania was opened at Harrisburg on the 6th of January, 1846, there was a large and influential lobby on hand to take part in the battle royal soon to open between diverse interests seeking to control a large share of the trade of the Ohio and Mississippi Valleys for the seaboard cities which those interests represented . . . It was a contest between two great cities—the one situated on the banks of the Delaware River, the other washed by the waters of the Patapsco—both desiring each for itself to procure a line of railroad to connect it with the forks of the Ohio. The latter had as an ally a formidable array of citizens of the southwestern counties of Pennsylvania, who, deeming themselves badly treated in the matter of internal improvements, and which treatment they attributed to Philadelphia, were clamorous for a rail line to the southern city . . . Philadelphia, aroused by the decadence of its internal trade, also appeared at the doors of the legislative bodies and asked for authority to build a line from Harrisburg to Pittsburgh. Bills for both projects were introduced in the legislature, and pressed steadily day by day. On the floor of the two houses, in the lobby, under the dome of the Capitol, in the hotel entries, along the board walk, at boarding houses, at all hours of day and night the friends of one or other of the measures buttonholed the members in advocacy or assailment. The contest at times became very acrimonious, and the debates teemed with adjectives of praise or denunciation. I, 3, 4.

capitalization and at least $1,000,000 paid in capital stock, and if at least fifteen miles of railway lines at each end of the projected line was completed by February 25, 1847, the right of way granted the Baltimore & Ohio Railroad would be canceled. The city of Philadelphia subscribed $2,500,000, the county of Allegheny $1,000,000, and private investors with Philadelphia commercial interests as their motivation subscribed the remainder. The necessary track mileage was completed, and the Pennsylvania Railroad received the coveted right of way.[35]

By 1873 the Pennsylvania Railroad had grown into the most powerful line in Pennsylvania.[36] Its mileage within the state, owned and leased, totaled 2,328 miles and roads and equipment were valued at $160,000,000. It reported the carriage of eighteen million passengers and of twenty-eight million tons of freight. Gross earnings for the year ran to $62,672,000 and expenditures to $41,246,000. Pennsylvania Railroad stock paid a 10 per cent dividend, half in cash and half in scrip. Subsidiary lines varied in dividends paid, some paying 6, 7, 8 and 10 per cent.[37]

The Philadelphia & Reading Railroad, ranking next in power and importance, owned 471 miles of track and leased an additional 260 miles; its roadbed and equipment represented a $73,000,000 investment. In 1873 it hauled seven million passengers and twelve million tons of freight. Its gross income slightly exceeded $15,000,000 and its expenses ran to less than half its costs. The Philadelphia & Reading paid a 10 per cent dividend in cash; dividends paid by its subsidiaries varied from 3½ per cent to 12 per cent.[38]

There were numerous independent lines still surviving in the commonwealth, many of them relatively short in length. Most of them were in the coal regions. Together, however, they represented considerable mileage and investment. Many of them extended beyond Pennsylvania

---

[35]*Ibid.*, pp. 27-28; Isaac Sharpless, *Two Centuries of Pennsylvania History*, J. B. Lippincott Co., 1900, p. 327.

[36]For a detailed description of this growth see Charles Burgess and Miles Kennedy, *Centennial History of the Pennsylvania Railroad Company*, especially chs. 11-22; a less comprehensive survey is contained in Howard W. Schotter, *The Growth and Development of the Pennsylvania Railroad Company*, pp. 58-119. At the beginning of the decade the Pennsylvania Railroad had 367 miles of track and revenues of almost $6,000,000.

[37]Commissioner of Pennsylvania Bureau of Industrial Statistics, *Second Annual Report*, 1873-74, table, pp. 88-89. The Pennsylvania Railroad also owned 573 miles of main line outside the state valued at over $60,000,000, included in operational statistics.

[38]*Ibid.*, table, p. 90.

borders. With an impressive 2,169 in the state and 1,000 outside, the independents were valued at over $324,000,000. They carried almost fifteen million passengers and approximately 42,000,000 tons of freight. Their gross receipts exceeded that of the Pennsylvania, totaling $67,-500,000; their expenses ran $48,750,000. Their dividend record was spotty. One line paid a 20 per cent dividend! Several paid 6 to 10 per cent, but many paid none at all.[39]

Undoubtedly the growth of railroads was essential for the industrial health of the state, and the consolidations resulting from the purchasing and leasing of smaller lines by the great railroad corporations promoted more efficient operation and management. There were, nevertheless, many criticisms and widespread misgivings regarding the railroad giants. The *Pittsburgh Gazette* in a leading editorial stated that the "great evil of the present system of railway management is that these corporations seek to control the actions of the Legislature and even of Congress, and their aim is to become a power greater than the Government itself. This is after all the real danger.... We fully believe that the time has come for the government to intervene in regard to railroad management ... to render more clear that the people, as well as the corporations, are parties in interest, with rights that ought to be respected."[40] Not only did the railroads make use of the lobby, but their attorneys were elected to the legislature and took part directly in legislation.

There were criticisms, also, of the use made of this political power. Some railroads had gained, by grace of the legislature, unlimited power to buy real estate and to hold it in perpetuity. The only limit, said the *Gazette*, "was the ability to buy."[41]

There were complaints, also, about inequalities in rates in favor of coal and manufactures owned by the same men who owned the railroads, and discriminations in favor of through freight. There were charges that both passengers and freight were carried from New York to Chicago at a much lower rate than between points in Pennsylvania.[42] Commenting on the Pennsylvania Railroad Report of 1873 filed with the Auditor General in March of that year, the *Pittsburgh Gazette* pointed out the significance of local traffic in the total business of that line. "Of the gross amount of tonnage for that year," said the editor, "take off such

---

[39]*Ibid.*, table, pp. 91-93. This includes mileage in Pennsylvania of out of state lines.
[40]Editorial, "Railroads and Government," March 27, 1873.
[41]*Pittsburgh Gazette*, April 17, 1873. See also Minority Report of Committee on Railroads, *Debates*, III, 407.
[42]*Pittsburgh Gazette*, Nov. 11, 1872; *ibid.*, April 21, 1873.

Pennsylvania products as coal, petroleum, iron, etc., and there would not be much left of its big business." Through traffic accounted for but one-seventh of its freight tonnage, and the disparity between through and local passenger service was even greater.[43] This added to the enormity of the offense of discriminating in favor of through transit.

There were criticisms directed against the Pennsylvania Railroad and other railroads with lines extending into other states that they made money in Pennsylvania and spent it on developments out of the state. This does not exhaust the list of sins alleged against the railroads! They were charged with responsibility for their share of guilt in the abuse of special legislation.

While the convention was in session, the Pennsylvania Railroad, anticipating the prohibition of special legislation in the future, rushed through the legislature a bill authorizing that railroad corporation to increase its capital stock and to borrow by the issuance of bonds secured by mortgage on the property and franchises of the company. The bill contained no limitation as to amount or purpose. The *Pittsburgh Gazette*,[44] commenting editorially on this action, stated that the bill was a "set-up" measure, that the railroad company had had an assured majority before the bill was introduced. Though the bill did not specify the purpose for the proposed increase in capital and indebtedness, Col. Noyes of Clinton explained on the floor of the House that the company wanted to lay four tracks between Pittsburgh and Philadelphia.[45] The measure was passed without dissent.

The *Pittsburgh Gazette* called upon the Governor to protect public interest by vetoing the bill. The following week Governor Hartranft did give notice to the legislative leaders that he would not approve the bill without limitations on the use of the new capital, and Senator Rutan introduced a resolution for the recall of the bill for purposes of revision. The bill was then passed in a modified form and approved by the governor.[46] The act authorized an increase of capital stock from $75,000,000 to $150,000,000 and its bonded indebtedness from $33,000,000 to $150,000,000.[47] Thus, the Pennsylvania Railroad[48] took advantage

---

[43] The *Gazette* carried the text of the Annual Report on Mar. 19, 1873; the editorial comment appeared on Mar. 5, 1873.
[44] Editorial entitled "Pennsylvania Railroad Bill," Feb. 10, 1873. The *Gazette* also pointed out that no reports of the introduction of the bill were printed in any other paper before passage of the bill, and that this was not "an accidental omission."
[45] *Pittsburgh Commercial*, Feb. 6, 1873.
[46] *Pittsburgh Gazette*, Feb. 18, 1873; *Pittsburgh Commercial*, Feb. 18, 1873.
[47] 1873 Pa. P. L. 99, signed by Governor Hartranft, Feb. 18, 1873.
[48] *Pittsburgh Gazette*, Mar. 5, 1873.

of its last chance to obtain "special legislation" by manipulation of state legislators.

In spite of the tremendous growth in manufacturing, heavy industry, and the extractive industries which marked this period, Pennsylvania remained an important agricultural state. Agricultural investments totaling $1,200,000,000[49] far exceeded investments in any other field except the steel industry and railroads. In 1870, Pennsylvania ranked fourth among the states in value of all farm products.[50] It ranked among the first five states in production of twelve major crops, and among the first ten in production of three others.[51] It ranked fourth in value of livestock; meat products for the year were valued at $28,500,-000. Farm wages represented an income of over $23,000,000.[52] The value of all farm products represented one-fourth of total production of the state. Pennsylvania not only fed its own people but exported from the port of Philadelphia $5,500,000 in breadstuffs and an additional $1,250,000 in agricultural provisions. This was the equivalent of more than one-sixth of the value of all exports from Philadelphia, which totaled $30,000,000.[53]

Although, as already recited, this was a remarkable period of economic growth, the fruits of economic expansion did not result in abundance for all. The Commissioner of Labor Statistics, commenting on the Ninth Census Report of 1870, stated:[54]

There is in the State of Pennsylvania a horde of laborers, constituting an army in numbers greater than that of the Potomac when its ranks were fullest, who live and rear their families, in some way, on an average income of less than $400 a year.

The Census figures show that there were 1,020,543 persons gainfully employed in Pennsylvania, or two out of every five persons over ten years of age. Of these, approximately 39,000 were children between the ages of ten and fifteen, or 6 per cent of the children of this age level.[55] There were over 19,000 children under sixteen employed in manufac-

---

[49]The 1870 Census values Pennsylvania farms at $1,044,000,000; farm implements, at $35,600,000; and livestock, at $115,600,000 (figures given in round numbers). *Ninth Census*, 1870, III, 81, 82.

[50]*Pittsburgh Gazette*, June 2, 1872. New York, Illinois and Ohio outranked Pennsylvania. The total value of farm production stood at $184,000,000. *Ninth Census*, III, 82.

[51]*Ninth Census*, III, 83, 84.

[52]*Ibid.*, p. 83.

[53]"Pennsylvania in its Industrial Aspects," *loc. cit.*, p. 263.

[54]*Loc. cit.*, p. 518.

[55]*Loc. cit.*, p. 9. This included 29,000 boys and 10,000 girls.

turing, the equivalent of one out of every sixteen so employed.[56] Approximately 927,000 were men and women between the ages of fifteen and sixty,[57] and the remaining 55,000, of course, were men and women over sixty years of age. Only 2,700 of these were women.[58]

Philadelphia and Pittsburgh were, of course, centers of thriving manufactures and accounted for a considerable portion of the working force of the state. In Philadelphia, 217,685 were reported as gainfully employed at the time of the 1870 census.[59] Of these 7,684, or slightly over 3 per cent, were children between the ages of ten and fifteen years.[60] The girls were employed mainly in light manufactures or as domestic servants.[61] The great bulk of the work force was, of course, drawn from the sixteen to fifty-nine years age group, 202,127, with a ratio of three to one of men as compared with women. Most of the women were employed either in garment manufactures or as domestics.[62] These two categories of employment accounted for 84 per cent of all employed women. About 1,500 of the remainder were teachers, and an additional 1,400 were employed as laundresses. There were 6,655 men and 1,209 women in the sixty and above age group who were employed. Women in this age group were employed almost exclusively as domestics or laundresses, though a few were employed in manufacturing.

In Pittsburgh there were 29,854 gainfully employed reported in the

---

[56]*Ninth Census*, III., 562. There were, however, 725,000 children in attendance at school. *Ibid.*, I, 426.

[57]805,000 men and 122,000 women, Commissioner of Pennsylvania Bureau of Industrial Statics, *Second Annual Report*, p. 49.

[58]By adjusting the figures given in the 1870 census to take into account the average number of days actually employed in the various categories of employment, the Commissioner of Labor Statistics arrived at the following condensed table:

Type of worker	Number Employed	Yearly Earnings
Foremen and full time hands	29,848	$737.70
Skilled workmen with families	135,786	571.47
Skilled workmen, single	25,726	545.61
Laborers with families	169,665	398.78
Laborers, single	56,555	346.95
Women and girls, single	11,656	230.53
Youths, self-supporting	10,365	151.79

Ibid., p. 518.

[59]*Ninth Census*, I, table XXXII, p. 794.

[60]There were 5,108 boys and 2,576 girls reported as employed.

[61]Domestic servants, 893; manufacturing (primarily clothing manufacturers), 1,567; clerks and saleswomen, 80.

[62]Manufacturing, 21,292; domestics, 21,059.

same census. The proportion of women and girls gainfully employed was much lower in Pittsburgh than in Philadelphia. There were 1,083 boys between the ages of ten and fifteen employed, but only 198 girls. Most of the girls were employed as domestic servants, only forty finding employment in manufactures. Of the 27,815 in the fifteen to fifty-nine age category only 4,018 were women. About a fourth of these were employed in light manufactures, and the remainder primarily as domestic servants. The sixty and above age group accounted for but 758 of the work force, and but 32 of these were women. The predominance of heavy industry in the Pittsburgh district accounts for the difference between the two areas in the employment of women and girls.[63]

Lorin Blodgett, who made a very detailed census of economic and social conditions in Philadelphia in the census year, reported that about 140,000 of Philadelphia's work force were employees on a wage basis, and they worked for about 9,000 employers or proprietors. Their wages in that year exceeded $62,000,000, an increase of $35,000,000 from the 1860 level with an increase of but one-third in the work force. Their wages equaled about 20 per cent of the value of products produced.[64] Wages for women in the power-loom factories producing cotton and woolen goods, where employment of women was high, paid from $7 to $14 a week. Girls and boys, employed at light tasks, were paid from $2 to $3.50 a week. In spite of Census figures on the number of persons under sixteen employed, Mr. Blodgett declared that it was "rare that grinding poverty compels premature employment." Not only were the tasks light, but employment was generally interrupted for several months each year.

In the heavy work of manufacturing men only were employed. Conditions were generally good, and "nothing is heard of strikes, or of hostility between proprietor and workmen." At one time men were paid about double the rate paid women, but the gap in wages had been narrowed by 1870, the ratio being about three to two. Wages and employment were generally good from the Civil War until 1867, but fell slightly during 1868 and 1869. This trend had been reversed in 1870. Many men were paid as much as $21 per week. Mr. Blodgett took considerable pride in the fact that with all its growth of industry and population, Philadelphia had remained a city of single-home dwellings, and that its

---

[63]*Ninth Census, loc. cit.*

[64]There were variations dependent upon whether the plant used steam power or relied wholly upon human energy. In plants without steam horsepower, 35 to 40 per cent of the value of the product was paid in wages; plants with steam power using costly materials paid out from 12½ per cent to 15 per cent of the value in wages.

work force was not housed in crowded tenements. He spoke confidently of the future. "The whole body of productive establishments is full of life and progress, new and magnificent structures are daily rising to be filled with new machinery...."[65]

Henry George, who made a firsthand study of labor conditions in the Pennsylvania coal mines in the 1880's painted a very bleak picture of the living conditions of the miners, both in anthracite and bituminous areas. Most miners, he found, were lodged in "dreary, monotonous rows of company houses." Most such houses were complete strangers to paint on the outside and unfinished on the inside. They were divided by thin partitions into two to four tenements of from two to four small rooms.[66] Here the miners and their families lived under the uncertainties of a lease subject to a five-day eviction notice.[67]

The general level of wages was low, and rendered less adequate by the irregularity of employment. Wages were paid largely in rental of company tenements and in goods furnished at company stores. The latter were commonly called "pluck me" stores by the miners, because prices were much higher than in non-company stores.[68] The most tragic testimony to the inadequacy of wages was the large number of boys employed at the mines at a tender age. It was not unusual for boys of seven or eight to go to work as slate pickers, working from 7 A.M. until dark under intolerable conditions. All day long they would sit, bent almost double, watching for and picking out with swift fingers any slate from the coal moving past them on the chute. By the time they were fifteen or sixteen, they were ready to go to work in the mines.[69] Census figures indicate that there were 9,051 "boys" employed by the anthracite mines

---

[65]Lorin Blodgett, "The Census of Industrial, Employment, Wage and Social Conditions in Philadelphia in 1870" address before the Philadelphia Social Science Association, April 23, 1872, printed in the annual *Report of* the Pennsylvania Bureau of Industrial Statistics, 1872-73, pp. 426, ff.

[66]Henry George, "Labor in Pennsylvania," *North American Review*, CXLIII, 165-182. He described living conditions in these terms: "The mere aspect of the hamlets that in the anthracite fields of Pennsylvania stretch out of the 'tall breakers,' or in the bituminous regions cluster around the tipples, is to the last degree dreary and forbidding, even in the early summer.... The impression that they give is of a dull, monotonous struggle for mere existence; of human life reduced to little more than animal terms, and shorn of all that gives it dignity, grace and zest." *Ibid.*, p. 172.

[67]Generally, they were required to sign "cut-throat" leases under which they waived the laws enacted to protect them, *ibid.*, p. 172.

[68]From 15 to 100 per cent higher; 25 to 40 per cent was the average excess charge, *ibid.*, p. 176.

[69]It was unlawful to employ children under ten, but the law was not enforced, *ibid*, p. 172.

and 334 in the bituminous mines in 1870.[70] They were paid 50 to 60 cents a day, but many of them had to travel some distance over company rails, for which they paid ten cents a trip. If they found the mine closed, the fare had to be paid anyway, and some boys, at times, found themselves in debt to the company. The Pennsylvania Commissioner of Labor Statistics estimated that the average annual income for boys employed by the mines in 1870 was $132.21. Adult laborers in the anthracite mines earned from $382.70 to $436.37 for the same year; skilled workmen, $546.71; and mine bosses and full-time hands made about $900.[71]

Already there were the beginnings of labor organization among the miners. During the Civil War, when the price of coal was high and employment was expanding, the Miners' and Laborers' Benevolent Association had succeeded in negotiating an agreement which had improved conditions for the miners, but this expired in 1871. The economic decline brought with it lower wages, and the increasing irregularity of employment in the early 1870's brought with it a renewal of the terrorism of the "Molly Maguires" that had almost disappeared during the more "prosperous" period.[72] Labor unions had been kept weak by the "conspiracy laws" under which strikes were regarded as unlawful conspiracies. In 1869, however, an act was passed which recognized the legality of labor organizations for "mechanics, journeymen, tradesmen and laborers"; and in 1872 the right to strike was legalized provided that wages were inadequate, or treatment was brutal or offensive, or union members were required to violate union rules. The act did not protect workers who sought to hamper those persons wishing to work.[73]

This economic expansion was, as one would expect, accompanied by a remarkable growth in population. The population of the state increased by 21 per cent during the decade, bringing the total population to an impressive three and a half million by 1870.[74] Population growth

---

[70]*Second Annual Report,* Pennsylvania Commissioner of Industrial Statistics, 1873-74, p. 469.

[71]*Ibid.,* 478.

[72]Nelson M. Bortz, Senior Economist, National Mediation Board, "The Molly Maguires," *The Pennsylvanian,* 1:9-10. It was not until the trial and conviction of nineteen, who were hanged for murder, and of others who were convicted and imprisoned in 1874 and 1875, that this terrorism ended. These convictions, says Bortz, "terminated one of the most violent eras in Pennsylvania's industrial development, but contributed little or nothing to the solution of the causes which had goaded the Mollies to desperate deeds."

[73]Act of May 8, 1869; Act of June 14, 1872. Court interpretation by the Common Pleas Courts in the coal area rendered these laws almost meaningless. Henry George, *op. cit.,* p. 273.

[74]*Ninth Census,* I, 3.

was not even throughout the state; the newly developing industrial centers, the coal and oil areas, experienced the highest rate of growth, the consequence in part of a steady flow of European immigrants to the areas of economic opportunity. Philadelphia, with a population of 674,000, ranked second only to New York City in size, but its rate of growth during the decade was slightly below that of the state.[75] The remaining cities among Pennsylvania's top ten, though smaller in size, experienced a spectacular growth.[76] Pittsburgh, with a population of 86,000 ranked sixteenth in the United States. Allegheny, Reading, and Scranton were included in the fifty largest cities in the country.[77] The part played by immigration in the growth of Pennsylvania cities is suggested by the large number of foreign born in the commonwealth's two largest cities. In Philadelphia 27.3 per cent of its residents were foreign born[78], and in Pittsburgh, 32.5.[79] The anthracite region also felt the expansive surge. Luzerne County grew by more than 77 per cent; Northumberland by 43 per cent; Schuylkill by 30 per cent; and Carbon County by 34 per cent. Venango County, important center of oil development, increased by 48 per cent.[80]

In judging the social implications of the era, the growth of public education cannot be ignored. Although it is true that there were 39,000 children under sixteen who were employed, it is nevertheless true that at the same time there were 725,000 children attending public schools.[81] Census figures indicate, however, that there were 132,000 persons over ten years of age who could not read; the number who could not write was even greater, 222,000, of which 95,500 were foreign born.[82] A. K. McClure in summarizing his view of this era of development stated:[83]

---

[75]*Ibid.*, p. 254. The Commissioner of Industrial Statistics of Pennsylvania by projecting Philadelphia's 19 per cent rate of growth for succeeding decades as compared with New York City's 12 per cent growth, confidently predicted that the Quaker city would by 1900 edge New York out of first place! Pennsylvania would become the Empire state. *First Annual Report,* 1872-73, p. 6.

[76]The percentage of growth, with cities listed in order of size, was as follows: Philadelphia, 19.18; Pittsburgh, 147.83; Allegheny, 104.14; Reading, 46.48; Scranton, 280.5; Erie, 108.57; Harrisburg, 72.35; Wilkes-Barre, 305.92; Williamsport, 183.01; Allentown, 72.95. (Pa. Bureau of Industrial Statistics, *Report,* 1872-73, p. 16.)

[77]*Ninth Census Report,* I, 598.

[78]*Ibid.*, p. 254.

[79]*Ibid.*, p. 274.

[80]Pa. Bureau of Industrial Statistics, *op. cit.*, p. 15.

[81]*Ninth Census,* I, 426.

[82]*Ibid.*

[83]*Old Time Notes of Pennsylvania,* I, 536.

Fortunately the Civil War quickened our industries and invited corporate interests to harvest millions from our oil, our coal, our iron, our lumber and other channels of industry . . . and our great state in a single decade thereafter advanced more in the development of wealth, the diffusion of education, and in prosperity throughout all its channels of industry and trade, than it ever before advanced in half a century.

Politically the period was one of "boss" control at the state capital and of "ring" dominance in the large cities. Simon Cameron, after the Civil War, established his "dynasty" that controlled state politics for half a century and put the Republican party in control of the executive and legislative branches of the state government. Political dissatisfactions were expressed through the Liberal Republican movement which in 1872 threw its strength to the Democratic candidate for governor and to Greeley for President. The Republicans, however, swept the state by almost a 40,000 majority. Machine control in Philadelphia helped to magnify the Republican vote.

The rapid growth of cities resulted in a variety of problems—rapid growth of city public works, growth of local indebtedness, endless interferences with local government through legislative enactment. Philadelphians complained bitterly regarding agencies created by the legislature with authority to build public buildings or parks, manned by persons appointed at Harrisburg, but supported by taxes on Philadelphians. There were complaints in Pittsburgh of irregularities in handling public funds. Local papers blamed their ills upon the local "ring" which worked hand in hand with the greater "ring" at the state capital.

This period also was marked by agitation for various types of social reform. There was a strong temperance movement which forced through a laggard legislature a local option law in 1872. Woman suffrage organizations were active in advocating their cause, and even invaded the legislative galleries to demand recognition when the Assembly was considering the call for the constitutional convention. There were public discussions of the social implications of the growing dominance of the corporate structure of business.

It was against this background of economic growth, urban growth, corporate influence in government, boss control, and political excitement that the movement for revision developed. There were many who were convinced that the only remedy for existing problems lay in the overhauling of the constitutional system to put up road blocks against abuses.

CHAPTER 5: THE CALLING OF THE CONVENTION OF 1872-1873

In his annual message to the legislature on January 4, 1871,[1] Governor Geary expressed the growing popular demand for change when he appealed to the legislature to call a constitutional convention to revise the 1838 constitution. After four years' experience as chief executive of the commonwealth, during which he had had "abundant opportunity for careful observation," he stated, he had become convinced that a thorough revision of the constitution was essential. During the past thirty years, he observed, amendments had been added which had given the old constitution "an incongruous and sort of patchwork character."

The most serious problem requiring constitutional change, he stated, was the tremendous growth of local and special laws in areas which should be covered by general laws. The legislature had for many years passed a variety of laws regarding such matters as roads, bridges, schools, elections, and poor laws for counties and townships. This had been carried to such extremes that people moving from one county to another "frequently found themselves under entirely different laws." Judges and lawyers, likewise, found entirely different laws in different districts. "Practically the whole theory of our constitution and government," he declared, "is subverted and destroyed by the present system of local interference." Local laws presented by a local member generally were, by courtesy, accepted by the rest of the legislative members. This abuse could be cured only by a constitutional provision requiring such matters to be governed by general laws.

Similarly, the abuse of "special legislation" could be cured only by a like remedy. "Special legislation is the great and impure fountain of

---

[1] *Pennsylvania Archives,* fourth series, VIII, 1127-1131.

corruption, private speculation and public wrong," Governor Geary asserted. "It has become a reproach to republican government, and is one of the most alarming evils of the times."

The governor suggested several other areas of possible constitutional action which might be explored by the convention if called: change in the suffrage provisions to conform to the Fifteenth Amendment to the national Constitution; the question of minority representation; enlargement of the General Assembly; limitations on corporate powers; greater security for public funds; the need for a lieutenant-governor; method of choice of state administrative officers;[2] the change of elections from October to November to avoid the necessity for two elections in presidential election years.

In response to the leadership thus assumed by the governor, the legislature passed a law submitting to a referendum of the people the question of a call for a constitutional convention.[3] The referendum was held at the general state election on October 10, 1871. It was approved by the people by a vote of 328,000 to 70,000.[4] Only Berks and Greene counties voted against it, but the vote was very close in Fayette, Monroe, and Montgomery. In half a dozen others the vote was less than 2 to 1 in favor of the calling of the convention. In Allegheny and Philadelphia counties the victory for the convention was overwhelming.[5] The vote in Philadelphia was singularly light. Two years later in the special election on the ratification of the constitution more than 84,000 votes were cast as contrasted with the pitiful 17,300 in the referendum on the calling of the convention.

The legislature at its next session passed the necessary enabling legislation. The legislative act provided for the election of delegates at the October election in 1872.[6] The convention membership was set at 133: 99 to be elected from the senatorial districts, 28 from the state at large, and 6 elected at large from Philadelphia. In order to assure that the convention would not be dominated by one party with a consequent partisan revision, the legislature provided for a limited vote system. The

---

[2]Governor Geary suggested that the lieutenant-governor, the treasurer, and the superintendent of schools should be elected; all other administrative officers should be appointed by the governor.

[3]1871 Pa. P. L. 262, approved by Governor Geary, June 2, 1871.

[4]John A. Smull, *Rules and Decisions of the General Assembly of Pennsylvania*, 1872, pp. 302-3.

[5]In Allegheny County the vote was 22,644 for and 359 against; in Philadelphia County, 16,781 for and 523 against.

[6]1872 Pa. P. L. 53, approved by Governor Geary, April 11, 1872.

plan reportedly was designed by Charles R. Buckalew, who had been actively advocating proportional representation in his speeches as he stumped the state as Democratic candidate for governor. He, however, credited Harry White with its authorship.[7] According to the plan, in the election of senatorial district delegates three were to be elected from each district, but each elector would vote for two. In the election of the state delegates at large, each voter would vote for fourteen, and in the Philadelphia election of delegates at large, each voter would vote for three. Thus, not only would the Republicans and Democrats share equally the delegates-at-large, but in each senatorial district the minority party would be assured one of the three district delegates.

The vote on convention delegates took place at the regular October election when the electorate was concerned about the choice between the candidates for governor. This was an especially spirited contest between John F. Hartranft, the choice of the Cameron forces, and Charles R. Buckalew, Democratic candidate, who had also been endorsed by many of the Liberal Republican leaders. This election was viewed by party leaders as a trial of strength between the opposing forces in preparation for the presidential contest between Grant and Greeley in November. The election of convention delegates was thus overshadowed by these major political battles and received scant attention in the press prior to the election.

As was anticipated when the enabling legislation was passed the Republicans won a slight majority of delegates, but this was sufficient to give them control over the organization of the convention.[8]

The legislative act calling the convention provided that it should convene at Harrisburg on November 12, 1872.[9] Any constitution or amendments proposed by the convention should be submitted for popular approval at the general election,[10] and a majority vote of those

---

[7]At one point in the debates of the convention Wayne MacVeagh complained that, though the Republican party had rolled up a resounding 40,000 majority in the October election, this was cancelled out in the convention, where the limited vote scheme had reduced the Republicans to a bare majority. Buckalew in reply defended the scheme as one producing a body that had for the most part been free of partisanship; it had been accepted, at the time of passage, by both parties as fair and equitable. The majority party had been willing to accept an assured though a slight majority. It was in this speech that Buckalew referred to Harry White as author of the plan. *Debates,* IV, 345; 348-9.

[8]Editorial in the *Pittsburgh Gazette,* Oct. 18, 1872.

[9]Sec. 3 provided that the convention should convene the second Tuesday in November.

[10]Sec. 6.

voting on the constitution or amendments should be sufficient to ratify.[11] One third of the members of the convention could compel the separate submission of any amendment.[12]

The legislature imposed two limitations on the convention. It excepted from powers of the constituent assembly the Declaration of Rights of the constitution of 1838,[13] which, it declared, should remain forever inviolate. The convention was also forbidden to create separate courts of equity.[14] The legislature appropriated $500,000 to pay the costs of the convention.[15]

---

[11]Sec. 5.

[12]Sec. 4.

[13]Constitution of 1838, Art. IX.

[14]Sec. 4.

[15]Sec. 7 provided for a salary of $1,000 plus mileage to and from the convention, and an allotment for postage and stationery.

CHAPTER 6: WORK OF THE CONSTITUTIONAL CONVENTION: LEGISLATIVE, EXECUTIVE, JUDICIARY

There are certain cardinal questions in the work of this Convention of very great importance to us that we solve them rightly, and to the people that we present them in a form likely to meet with their acceptance. Upon them intelligent men differ greatly. . . . What should be the relation of the judiciary to a free state? What should be the relation of the state itself to the great monopolies of modern civilization? What are the best methods of representation to secure a just expression of the popular will compatible with strength of government? These and possibly one or two other matters of a similar character—what should be the limitations upon the granting of special favors by legislative action, and how best the lines may be drawn between the judgment of the courts and the judgment of legislative bodies in private controversies . . . are the questions today of grave and pressing import for the people of Pennsylvania; possibly, how the State in its corporate capacity can wisely interfere in aid of labor in its unequal struggle with capital, and possibly, I repeat, other questions as well, that are now pressing upon the attention of all thoughtful men engaged in laying anew the basis of organic law for large, industrious, thriving communities like Pennsylvania. WAYNE MAC VEAGH, *Debates*, I, 45.

THE convention assembled at Harrisburg on November 12, 1872. The evening before its official opening, Wayne MacVeagh, Republican leader of the Cameron faction, called a caucus of the Republican delegates to plan the organization of the convention, agree upon a ticket for convention officers, and plan strategy. They agreed to assign the Democrats some of the lesser posts.[1] The formal opening came at noon, when the constituent body was called to order by Francis Jordan, secretary of the commonwealth.

The convention was, indeed, an impressive gathering, including men who had distinguished themselves both on the state and national political scenes. William Bigler and A. G. Curtin were former governors of Pennsylvania.[2] Jeremiah Black, after a distinguished career as Chief Justice of the Pennsylvania Supreme Court, had served under Buchanan successively as United States Attorney General, Secretary of State and reporter of the United States Supreme Court.[3]

General William Meredith, who was elected president of the convention and served in that post until his death on August 17, 1873, had been United States Secretary of the Treasury, and had served as Attorney General of Pennsylvania from 1861-67.[4] Charles R. Buckalew had had a varied political career as state senator, United States diplomatic rep-

---

[1] *Pittsburgh Gazette*, Nov. 13, 1872. The *Gazette* commented favorably upon this action, but its Democratic opponent, the *Pittsburgh Post* carried some caustic comments by its Harrisburg reporter: "To the old dwellers at the State Capital like myself . . . all this is very amusing. But what amuses me most is the cool impudence of the Ring, which holds its regular sessions as usual, to map out the business of our honest friends of the Convention. The smooth and quasi son-in-law of the grand old ring-master (Cameron) . . . MacVeagh with the escaped Libby prisoner, White, are trying to run the concern. They made a ticket of officers Monday night at their caucus, which, as Mr. Cuyler very properly said, was most 'indecently' announced on the morning before the Convention met, to the newspapers. But Mr. Cuyler, guileless man, has not been here so long as I have. . . That was a very small part of their 'indecencies.'" Dispatch published Nov. 16, 1872. The caucus choice as chief clerk was ridiculed as incompetent.

[2] Governor Bigler was governor from 1852-55; he had also served in the United States Senate from 1856-62. At the time of his election to the convention he was President of the Philadelphia and Erie Railroad. Governor Curtin was the famous "war governor" of Pennsylvania, having served from 1861-67; he had also served as Secretary of the Commonwealth and Superintendent of Common Schools before his election as governor, and had served at one time as United States Minister to Russia. A. D. Harlan, *Pennsylvania Constitutional Convention 1872 and 1873*, pp. 37-38; p. 48.

[3] A. D. Harlan, *op. cit.*, pp. 38-39. As a state court judge he had been a vigilant defender of public interest against encroachment of corporate interests, especially railroads, on public interest; on the national legal scene he had been counsel for the petitioner in the famous *Ex Parte Milligan Case*. See William N. Brigance, *Jeremiah Sullivan Black*, p. 145, ff.

[4] A. D. Harlan, *op. cit.*, p. 28. President Meredith was seventy-three years of age and in very poor health at the time of his election as president of the convention. He was a very popular public figure, widely respected. His health prevented him from taking a very active part in the proceedings. The reporter of the *Pittsburgh*

resentative to Ecuador, United States Senator, and had been Democratic candidate for governor of Pennsylvania in the 1872 election. He was regarded as the chief spokesman for the Democratic forces in the convention.[5] Wayne MacVeagh, who had assumed leadership in the pre-convention caucus maneuvers, was regarded as the Republican leader. He was a leading member of the Pennsylvania bar and Republican state chairman. In 1881 he was appointed United States Attorney General.[6] George W. Woodward, who had taken an active part in the framing of the judiciary article in the preceding convention, was again a leading participant in debate on that article. He had served for ten years as President Judge of the Fourth Judicial District of Pennsylvania and fifteen years on the Pennsylvania Supreme Court bench, including a tour of duty as Chief Justice of the latter court.[7]

Six delegates had been members of Congress, about a score had served in the Pennsylvania legislature, half a dozen had held posts as heads of executive departments at Harrisburg, two had served as state Supreme Court judges, and many others had had experience as local government officials. Four of the delegates had been delegates to the 1837-38 constitutional convention: William Darlington, Judge Woodward, General Meredith, and Samuel Purviance.[8]

Of the 133 delegates 103 were lawyers.[9] This was not unusual for a

---

Gazette who was covering the convention for his paper described him thus: "He is a natty looking old gentleman, with close cropped hair, brilliant eye, stiff standing collar, closely buttoned coat, and carries a courteous and high bred air. He is evidently a man of the traditional old school." *Pittsburgh Gazette*, Nov. 13, 1872.

[5] A. D. Harlan, *op. cit.*, 41. Buckalew had also served as a district attorney in Columbia county, and, on appointment by Governor Packer, as Commissioner to revise the Penal Laws of the State. He was reelected to the state Senate in 1870, '71, '72 and '73. Senator A. K. McClure, liberal spokesman, who had served in the state Senate with him, said of him: "Charles R. Buckalew was one of the ablest men of the Democratic leaders of his time. He was not an organizer, he had little or no knowledge of political strategy, and was entirely unfitted for the lower strata methods of modern politics. He came to the senate [state] in 1852 hardly known outside his own district; he was singularly quiet and unobtrusive in manner, and never in any way sought to exploit himself. He won his position in the party solely by the great ability he possessed, his practical efficiency in legislation, and the absolute purity of his character. He was ordinarily a cold, unimpassioned speaker, but eminently logical and forceful." *Old Time Notes of Pennsylvania*, II, 39. Buckalew was author of a book on proportional representation, and an earnest advocate of that cause.

[6] A. D. Harlan, *op. cit.*, pp. 64, 65.

[7] A. D. Harlan, *op. cit.*, p. 89.

[8] *Pittsburgh Gazette*, Nov. 22, 1872.

[9] When the convention opened there were 101 lawyers, but the number was increased to 103 in the filling of vacancies.

nineteenth-century constituent assembly. In view of the impending struggle to curtail corporate powers with special attention to railroads, it is not surprising that such interests were well represented. One newspaper of the time commenting on such representation pointed out that there were between fifty and sixty lawyers for corporations serving as delegates.[10] Well represented among these were the great railroads. Franklin B. Gowen,[11] delegate-at-large, was president of the Philadelphia & Reading Railroad; ex-Governor Bigler[12] was president of the Philadelphia and Erie Railroad; E. C. Knight[13] and William H. Smith,[14] delegates-at-large, were both directors of the Pennsylvania Railroad and some lesser lines. Theodore Cuyler[15] also a delegate-at-large, was chief counsel for the Pennsylvania Railroad and had served on its legal staff for seventeen years. Gowen reportedly had with him eight or ten special attorneys for his line, elected from as many districts, and Cuyler, too, had special attorneys elected from various counties throughout the state. Other railroads also had their representatives.[16] Commenting wryly upon this situation the *Pittsburgh Gazette*[17] stated:

It is the presumption of course they are all honest Godfearing men, loving the State and abjuring evil ways, and that they have come here seriously ambitious of promoting the general welfare, and have left their special attorneyships in their upper desk drawers, not to be thought of in connection with their duties as constitutionalists.

The same paper, however, characterized the members of the convention as "generally men of intellect and culture, and in every way worthy to represent the great 'Keystone' in such an assembly."[18]

The convention organized by electing its president, William Morris Meredith, by unanimous vote, and by appointing the minor officers. Twenty-seven committees were appointed to conduct the preparatory drafting of proposals. In defiance of the legislatively imposed restrictions on its powers, the convention authorized a committee on Declaration of Rights.[19] Though the changes made in the Bill of

---

[10] *Ibid.*, Nov. 22, 1872.
[11] A. D. Harlan, *op. cit.*, p. 55.
[12] *Ibid.*, p. 38.
[13] *Ibid.*, p. 61.
[14] *Ibid.*, p. 82.
[15] *Ibid.*, p. 48.
[16] *Pittsburgh Gazette*, Nov. 22, 1872.
[17] *Loc. cit.*
[18] *Ibid.*, Nov. 13, 1872.

[19] The vote was 106 to 18 to establish the committee. *Debates of the Convention to Amend the Constitution of Pennsylvania*, 1872-1873 (hereafter cited as *Debates*), I, 61-62. The convention thus overwhelmingly, irrespective of party lines, "spat upon" the restriction of its substantive powers, as the *Pittsburgh Post* stated it. *Pittsburgh Post*, Nov. 20, 1872.

Rights were minor in character, this action of the convention became an important legal issue in the battle of its opponents to defeat it.

As one would expect, the chairmanship of most of the key committees were assigned to Republicans. Thus Wayne MacVeagh was awarded the chairmanship of the Committee on the Legislature and his close political colleague, Harry White, the chairmanship of the Committee on Legislation. These were regarded as the two crucial committees. Such distinguished Democrats as Curtin, Buckalew, Woodward, and Black could not be ignored. Curtin became chairman of the Committee on the Executive; Buckalew, of the Committee on Public and Municipal Debts and Sinking Funds; Woodward, of the Committee on Private Corporations; Black, of the Committee on Constitutional Sanctions.[20]

In its rules of debate the convention provided for three readings for all convention proposals. First reading would take place in the Committee of the Whole. No one could speak more than twice upon the same proposal.[21] After the convention had listened to some old-fashioned hour-long debates, it adopted a twenty-minute rule for debate in the Committee of the Whole.[22] At first it was relatively easy for a speaker to obtain unanimous consent to extend his remarks, but as the session wore on, objections became more frequent.

The convention met at Harrisburg until November 27. During this brief session it organized and adopted its rules, then recessed until January 7, when it met in Philadelphia. The change was necessitated by the return of the legislature to the state capital in January.

The convention got under way slowly. The proposals on suffrage and elections, the reports of the two committees on the legislative articles, and the judiciary article were the objects of prolonged discussion. Debates on first reading in the Committee of the Whole were not completed on all articles until late in June. With the coming of the hot summer months there was considerable absenteeism, and at times it was difficult to muster a quorum.[23] As completion of the long drawn-out debate on the first reading neared, the restless delegates seriously considered an adjournment for the summer months. A motion to recess

---

[20]*Journal of the Convention of 1872-73*, I, 89-90. There were three times as many standing committees as there had been in the convention of 1836-37. Each member served upon several committees.

[21]For the rules of the convention, see *ibid.*, pp. 56, ff.

[22]*Debates*, II, 308.

[23]Even as early as the middle of May the convention was experiencing difficulty at times in maintaining a quorum. See *Debates*, IV, 539-543; 554; 562; 594. Friday afternoon, Saturday and Monday morning sessions, especially, were delayed by difficulty in obtaining a quorum.

from June 27 to October 21 was introduced, but this was rejected by a vote of fifty-two to forty-three.[24] Not until most of the action on second reading had been completed did they recess from July 16 until September 16.[25] Third reading was not begun until September 25. By this time most argumentative issues had been settled in the spirit of compromise,[26] and third reading was completed by the end of October.[27] The report of the Committee on Revision and Adjustment (the convention's committee on style) was approved on November 1,[28] and the ordinance for the submission of the constitution to the people was adopted two days later.[29] The convention set December 16 as the date for the referendum. They provided for and appointed a special commission to administer the election in Philadelphia, but provided that the regular election officials should administer it elsewhere.[30] The constitution was submitted as a single unit for an affirmative or negative vote on the document as a whole, in spite of repeated attempts to force separate submission of the judiciary article.

The convention appointed an executive committee to look after any necessary action during recess of the convention,[31] instructed the Commission on Revision and Adjustment to prepare and publish for public distribution an exhibit of the changes proposed and an address to the people,[32] then recessed until December 27. The final session was held at that time for the purpose of canvassing the election returns on the ratification of the constitution.[33]

---

[24]*Debates*, V, 751. (The proposal was agreed to on June 20, but rescinded June 23). An editorial in the *Pittsburgh Commercial,* poking fun at the delegates, stated, "These distinguished and dignified gentlemen appear to entertain the roving thought that the work of making a Constitution for the state, with the thermometer among the 90's and 100's will have a direct tendency to impair their own feeble organisms." June 2, 1873.

[25]*Debates*, VI, 754.

[26]Exceptions were the lively debate on the railroad article, and the repeated attempts made by the opponents of the judiciary article to force the separate submission of this article at the popular referendum on the Constitution.

[27]By way of contrast, the debates on third reading, including the necessary action in preparation for the popular referendum on the Constitution, filled but one volume of the *Debates* (volume VIII), whereas the first reading fills four volumes, and second reading, three volumes.

[28]*Debates*, VIII, 681.

[29]*Debates*, VIII, 712.

[30]*Debates*, VIII, 703, 704. Sec. 1 and 4 of The Ordinance.

[31]*Debates*, VIII, 685, 697.

[32]*Debates*, VIII, 685.

[33]*Debates*, VIII, 697.

Legislative Branch

Each score of years we dole out to our legislators a fresh lease of power with increased restrictions, unwilling to trust them with more of Jove's power than is absolutely necessary to carry on the affairs of men while Jove nods. We are strongly inclined to think that this idea is a false one, and that it would be far preferable to grant almost unlimited powers to our representatives, and at the same time to hold them strictly responsible for their most trifling acts.

EDITOR, *The Penn Monthly*[34]

As already indicated, the primary concern of the convention was the correction of the evil practices in the enactment of legislation. To correct existing evils the constitution-makers used several devices. Foremost among these was the limitation of the powers of the legislature. Thus they forbade the General Assembly to pass special laws upon an enumerated list of subjects, twenty-seven in all, including grants of private and municipal charters.[35]

Frank Manton of Crawford County delivered the leading address in defense of the proposal when it was discussed in Committee of the Whole. After having given a statistical analysis of the bills passed during all legislative sessions from 1866-71 which indicated the overwhelming preponderance of special bills,[36] Mr. Manton pointed out that in that same period the legislature had passed 450 special acts bearing on railroads. This figure, impressive as it was, did not, he explained, indicate the full measure of railroad influence, for there were many other bills in which the railroads had had a direct or indirect interest. The only possible protection of public interest, he felt, lay in constitutional restriction.[37]

This proposal met with no marked opposition on the floor of the convention. With a few minor amendments it was agreed to in Com-

---

[34]"The Pennsylvania Constitutional Convention of 1872-73," *The Penn Monthly*, 4:(1873) 1-19, at 1.

[35]Art. III, Sec. 7.

[36]*Table of Laws passed 1866-1872:*

Date	General	Special	Date	General	Special
1866	50	1,096	1870	54	1,276
1867	86	1,392	1871	81	1,353
1868	73	1,150	1872	54	1,232
1869	77	1,276			
			Total	475	8,775

(Included in remarks of Frank Manton, *Debates*, II, 593.)

[37]*Debates*, II, 590-3.

mittee of the Whole[38] and accepted without significant revision on subsequent readings.[39]

The adoption of the proposal was not surprising; indeed, it had been generally assumed that the cutting off of the abuses that had grown up about special legislation would be the primary concern of the convention.

The convention not only limited the legislature to passage of general legislation upon the enumerated list, it also provided that special laws not so prohibited could be passed only after notice and publication.[40]

Numerous limitations were imposed also upon the substantive powers of the legislature. Thus, the legislature was forbidden by the constitution to levy taxes that are not uniform upon the same class of subjects.[41] The exemption of property from taxation was narrowly limited.[42] These provisions, though new, were accepted without debate when considered in Committee of the Whole and were approved by the convention without revision. There is, therefore, no indication as to whether the convention really intended to prohibit all forms of graduated taxes upon incomes and inheritances, though the requirement of uniformity has been so interpreted by the Pennsylvania Supreme Court.[43]

Circumscriptions regarding appropriations as well as taxes were also imposed. Thus a two-thirds vote in each house was required for the adoption of appropriation bills granting state funds to charitable or educational institutions not under state control.[44]

The convention not only limited the powers of the legislature, it

---

[38]*Debates*, II, 622.

[39]*Debates*, V, 248-265 records the action on second reading.

One delegate, J. McDowell Sharpe, referring back to this section when the limitations on appropriations for charitable purposes were under discussion, did say, "I lay no claim to the possession of prophetic ken, but I predict that the oldest member of this Convention will live to see the day when better experience will teach the people that this has been a mistake." *Ibid.*, II, 669.

[40]Art. III, Sec. 3; acted on in Committee of the Whole, *Debates*, II, 629.

[41]Art. IX, Sec. 1.

[42]Public property used for public purposes, actual places of worship, places of burial not operated for a profit, and institutions of "purely public charity" could be exempted, but no other property. Art. IX, Secs. 1 and 2.

[43]*American Stores Co. v. Boardman, Secretary of Revenue*, 336 Pa. 36 (1939).

[44]Art. III, Sec. 17, approved in Committee of the Whole, *Debates*, II, 698. The Committee on Legislation had proposed an even more stringent requirement of a three-fourths vote, but an amendment proposed by Mr. Buckalew reducing the requirement to a two-thirds vote was adopted by the Committee of the Whole.

also adopted many other restrictive devices. Thus it abandoned annual sessions for biennial sessions. The proponents of this change felt that the elimination of special legislation would leave the legislature with ample time to consider and pass the necessary general legislation. As one delegate pointed out, during the preceding six sessions 1,200 to 1,500 bills had been passed in each session, but not more than fifty general laws had been enacted in any session. Anyway, the less legislation, the better! Biennial sessions would be an improvement.[45] Furthermore, biennial sessions would give a longer period to test a law and make possible a more intelligent approach to any proposed revision or repeal.[46]

Summarizing the point of view of the committee which had prepared the legislative article, Wayne MacVeagh, chairman, stated that it was the considered judgment of the committee that biennial sessions were preferable, since "every statute that is passed introduces an element of change into relations existing between the citizens of this Commonwealth, and that change in the law is in itself an evil of considerable importance, and only to be justified by a clear advantage resulting from it." Furthermore, the committee felt that once every two years was often enough "for a civilized community to submit the whole body of its laws" to public officials chosen especially to make such changes. The elimination of special legislation would make it possible for the legislature to consider and pass all the general legislation necessary in a session of three months, once every two years.[47]

Other delegates pointed to the savings resulting from the elimination of sessions every other year. It cost $400,000 to hold a session![48] Still others reasoned that the break between sessions would weaken, if not eliminate, organized lobbies, since it would destroy the continuity of their activities.[49]

There were some, however, who raised their voices against the proposed change.[50] Among these was William M. Darlington, who

---

[45]Henry Carter, *Debates*, II, 359. Similar opinions were expressed by Hugh N. McAllister, *ibid.*, p. 368; Augustus S. Landis, *ibid.*, pp. 368-9; Thomas E. Cochran, *ibid.*, p. 383; and John M. Broomall. Cochran said the interior counties were very apprehensive about annual sessions.

[46]Samuel Minor, *Debates*, II, 359.

[47]*Debates*, II, 327.

[48]J. Price Wetherill, *Debates*, II, 333.

[49]Thomas R. Hazzard confidently predicted that the vocation of the lobbyist would end with the adoption of biennial sessions! *Debates*, II, 381-383.

[50]For text of Minority Report supporting annual sessions, see *Debates*, II, 283.

had been a delegate to the 1837 convention and regarded the constitution of 1838 with a considerable measure of veneration. He opposed this departure from tradition. What evils, he asked, were there that annually elected legislatures were subject to, to which biennially chosen bodies would not also be subject. If the legislature was a public nuisance and legislators were disturbers of the peace it were best that they should never meet. Biennial sessions would simply make a betrayal of trust more serious, for it would take the voters two years rather than one to remedy the evil by reversing the action of dishonorable legislators. Furthermore, annual sessions were necessary for a state the size of Pennsylvania, especially one with such diverse interests. "Can it be possible," he asked, "that for two years no portion of this great state would require particular legislation to advance its interests and develop its resources?" If any section or interest did need such legislation, should it be compelled to wait two years?[51]

David N. White, with a foresight which has been vindicated by experience, pointed out that biennial sessions would necessitate biennial budget appropriations with the accompanying difficulties in predicting two years ahead.[52] The advocates of change, however, prevailed, and biennial sessions were established.[53]

Still another method devised for purifying the legislative halls was the imposition of constitutional guarantees of regularity in procedure. Each restriction was designed to eliminate some alleged abuse in current procedure. Thus, the constitution provides that all laws must be passed in the form of a bill,[54] that no bills may be considered on the floor until reported out of committee and printed,[55] that all bills must have three readings at length on three separate days in each house,[56] that no bill may contain more than one subject,[57] and that every bill must have a title which clearly expresses the purpose of the bill.[58] All

---

[51] William Darlington, *Debates* II, 356-7; George W. Biddle also spoke at length in support of annual sessions, *ibid.*, pp. 364-8; John H. Walker denounced biennial sessions as a means of removing from the people control over their government, *ibid.*, 373. Charles Buckalew supported annual sessions combined with two year terms, *ibid.*, p. 359.

[52] *Debates*, II, 393.

[53] Art. II, Sec. 4.

[54] Art. III, Sec. 1. This was carried over from the 1838 Constitution.

[55] Sec. 2.

[56] Sec. 4.

[57] Sec. 3.

[58] *Ibid.*

bills passed by either chamber must be signed by the presiding officer in the presence of the members of that house.[59] These were adopted with little debate.

There was also a vigorous struggle to purify the legislature by requiring members to take an "iron clad" oath before entering office.[60] Both the Committee on the Legislature and the Committee on Legislation proposed a detailed oath.[61] In both versions each member of the legislature was required to swear or affirm that he had been guilty of no corruption in gaining his victory at the polls and that he had not and would not accept any bribe or permit private solicitation of his vote in the legislature. Wayne MacVeagh of Dauphin County, chairman of the Committee on the Legislature, in an eloquent address defended the proposal of his committee.[62] Judge Jeremiah Black on the occasion of debate on the proposal of the Committee on Legislation delivered a fiery speech cataloguing the sins of the legislators, portraying their betrayal by corporate interests, and describing the railroad corporations as the master betrayers.[63] All those who supported the "iron clad" oath insisted that the oath should be specific in nature so that any legislator who betrayed his trust could be prosecuted for perjury.[64] Judge Black wished to go a step further. He felt that legislators also should be required to give under oath an accounting of their conduct in office. Just as an administrator or guardian is required to give under oath an accounting of his fulfillment of his trust, so the legislator at

---

[59]Sec. 9.

[60]The length of debate attests to its vigor: 93 double-columned pages!

[61]Both the Committee on the Legislature and the Committee on Legislation reported proposed oaths for the legislators. The oath proposed by the Committee on the Legislature follows: "I do solemnly swear (or affirm) that I will support the Constitution of the United States and the Constitution of the State of Pennsylvania, and will faithfully discharge the duties of Senator (or Representative) according to the best of my ability and I do solemnly swear (or affirm) that I have not paid or contributed anything, or made any promise in the nature of a bribe, to corrupt or influence, directly or indirectly, any vote at the election at which I was chosen to fill the said office; and I do further solemnly swear (or affirm) that I have not accepted or received, and that I will not accept or receive, directly or indirectly, any money or other valuable thing from any corporation, company or person for any vote or influence I may give or withhold on any bill, resolution or appropriation, or for any other official act." The proposal of the Committee on Legislation was similar. *Debates*, I, 453; II, 485.

[62]*Debates*, I, 463-66; the proposal was also supported by Thomas Howard, *Debates*, I, 471.

[63]*Debates*, II, 485-493.

[64]For debates see *Debates*, I, 453-471; II, 485-560.

the end of the session should be required to swear that he had not violated the constitution, had not listened to private solicitations, taken any bribe, or committed any act in his official capacity in violation of the law![65] This latter oath the Judge regarded as more efficacious than the first.[66]

William Darlington in an eloquent speech implored the convention to refrain from so degrading the legislators. Why, he asked, should an honest man be required to swear he is not a rogue? He urged that all officers should be required to take a common oath to support the constitution[67] and that the legislators should not be singled out as potential criminals. John Walker indignantly asserted that "no man who feels as a man, who acts as a man, who is a man . . . can think of such an oath without feeling his manhood insulted."[68]

The separate oath for legislators was ultimately abandoned, but the oath of office required of all elective state officers embodied most of the principles of the "iron clad" oath.[69] Judge Black's proposal for an "accounting" at the end of public service was, however, rejected. This the Judge regarded as a signal victory for the forces of unrighteousness.

There was also extended debate regarding apportionment of representation. This reflected the conflict of interest between Philadelphia and the rest of the state in regard to the arrangement for senatorial apportionment, and of rural interest against city interests in respect to representation in the House of Representatives.

The constitution of 1838 had limited city representation in the Senate by providing that no city or county should have more than four members in the Senate. Originally, Philadelphia City had sent four senators and the county one, but when the two were consolidated, the representation in the Senate was reduced to four out of thirty-three. Thus Philadelphia, with one-fifth of the population of the state, had but one-eighth of the representation. The 1870 census revealed a considerable disparity in ratio of representation from senatorial district to

---

[65]*Debates*, II, 491-492.

[66]*Debates*, II, 493.

[67]*Ibid.*, I, 467, 469. A similar position was presented by James Newlin, who proposed members should be required simply to swear that they would support the Constitution of the United States and of Pennsylvania, and carry out their duties with fidelity. I, 454; 459.

[68]*Ibid.*, I, 374.

[69]Art VII. By way of contrast, the 1838 Constitution simply required such officers to take an oath (or affirmation) "to support the constitution of this commonwealth, and to perform the duties of their respective offices with fidelity." Constitution of 1838, Art. VIII.

senatorial district. Thus, for Philadelphia, the representation figure was one senator for each 168,500; for Allegheny County, one for 87,400; for Montgomery, one for 81,600; for Fayette and Greene counties, one for 69,000. The delegates from Philadelphia pled with the convention to remove the discrimination against their city. The true basis of representation, they insisted, was population. All Philadelphia asked for was fairness, nothing more. Philadelphia was growing so rapidly that the inclusion in the constitution of an absolute maximum became more discriminatory year by year. Why, they asked, should a community which paid $2,500,000 of the state's $7,000,000 in tax revenues be denied an appropriate voice in the councils of government?[70]

Judge Woodward rose to defend the principle of limitation of great city representation. The principle had been written into the 1838 constitution under the leadership of Thaddeus Stevens after a dramatic clash between Stevens and William M. Meredith, cast in the role of chief defender of the rights of Philadelphia. The people had approved the limitation, and, declared Woodward, they "will never give it up while the world stands, and it never ought to be given up." Population, he granted was the appropriate basis for representation, but great cities were an exception. It would be a serious error to give unrestricted representation to "our overgrown communities." Experience indicated that great cities did not send to the legislature men who represented "the intellect, culture and enterprise" of the community. Most of the vicious legislation at Harrisburg had come from the great cities.[71]

Cities, after all, Woodward declared, depend upon rural areas for the source of their strength. The prosperity of the state as a whole rests upon the labor of the people in the rural communities. Philadelphia was, indeed growing rapidly, so rapidly, in fact, that it would soon control the legislature if no restriction was imposed on its representation. The farmer, upon whose products the cities live, would never permit it. After all, cities depend upon the rural areas for their existence, and not rural areas upon cities.[72]

Wayne MacVeagh, though speaking with more restraint than the voluble judge, supported the same general position. Either you must disfranchise the city to some extent, he stated, or else you must dis-

---

[70] See remarks of Mr. Worrell, *Debates*, II, 171; Mr. Campbell, *ibid.*, p. 173; Mr. Wetherill, *ibid.*, pp. 170-172; Mr. Knight, *ibid.*, p. 173; Mr. Simpson, *ibid.*, pp. 175-176; Mr. Biddle, *ibid.*, p. 180; Mr. Littleton, *ibid.*, pp. 181, 182; Mr. Stanton, *ibid.*, pp. 186-187.

[71] *Debates*, II, 173-175.

[72] *Debates*, II, 177-181. Though now a resident of Philadelphia, Woodward's views doubtless reflected his long residence in Luzerne County.

franchise the country; if Philadelphia were given full representation, it would be impossible to preserve the rights of the country. City delegations can more effectively organize, and thus have a more effective voice in the legislative chambers than an equal number of members from rural counties. For this reason the eighteen representatives and four senators from Philadelphia, sitting in the two houses, have at least three times as much influence as the like number from elsewhere. Upon all local matters Philadelphia representatives stand together. Without a constitutional limitation on their representation they, he declared, would control everything.[73]

Corroborating this position, other delegates pointed out the extent of Philadelphia influence at Harrisburg. As a delegate from one of the interior counties stated it, Philadelphia had had control of every important committee from time immemorial. There had been no committee on railroads or corporations for twenty years not created at the behest of its representatives, no speaker chosen without their assent. If Philadelphia had suffered at all, it was not by virtue of the constitutional limitation on numbers, but from negligence in the choice of its representatives.[74] Another delegate[75] declared that Philadelphia and Pittsburgh controlled the legislature. The speaker and the clerk of the House of Representatives were Philadelphians, and the speaker and clerk of the Senate were from Pittsburgh; all other important offices were shared between them. The rest of the state were "nothing but hewers of wood and drawers of water for these immense cities." Yet another delegate defended the departure from exact numerical representation as justified because experience indicated that "wherever in the world there is concentration—and I use the word in its strongest form—a concentration of wealth, a concentration of population, a concentration of commercial interests, a concentration of manufacturing interests, a concentration of railroad interests, and of other interests that might be enumerated, by virtue of this very concentration they acquire power and influence that the same interests and population would not have if scattered throughout many communities."[76]

The practices of other states and nations were cited to substantiate the principle underlying the limitation. Thus, in Great Britain, London

---

[73] *Debates*, II, 206.

[74] John S. Mann of Potter County, *Debates*, II, 209, 210.

[75] Daniel Kaine of Fayette County, *Debates*, II, 219-220.

[76] Samuel Minor of Crawford County, *Debates*, II, 206-208; a similar position was taken by John A. Purviance, *ibid.*, pp. 211, 212.

and other cities had restricted representation; so, likewise, Boston, Baltimore, Providence, and Charleston (N. C.).[77] Also, it was pointed out, there was no restriction on numbers in the House of Representatives. Why have two houses if the representation in both was to be identical?[78] Besides members of the legislative body are chosen to legislate for the whole community. With special legislation eliminated, there would be no need for such jealous protection of Philadelphia rights as had been necessary under the old system of local legislation.[79] Though one might suppose that Allegheny County, and especially Pittsburgh, with its fast-growing population, would have supported Philadelphia, some of the bitterest attacks came from the Allegheny County delegation. Pittsburgh was still smarting from the defeat in the struggle two decades earlier when the Pennsylvania won out over the Baltimore & Ohio in regard to the western extension of the railroad.[80]

The loyal sons of Philadelphia rallied to defend her. They protested indignantly against the characterization of their great city as an unproductive consumer, bent upon a grasp for power to be used for selfish ends. They denied the validity on democratic grounds of any alleged principle that would exclude cities from fair representation. They pointed to the manner in which cities had suffered from legislative interference and demanded as an alternative to acceptance of equitable representation the right to control their own affairs.[81]

After the debate had ruffled tempers for two days, a motion was made by a Philadelphia delegate that the restrictive provision should be stricken out, but this was defeated.[82] As finally written into the constitu-

---

[77] Jerome B. Niles of Tioga County, *Debates*, II, 229-231.

[78] J. McDowell Sharpe of Franklin County, *Debates*, II, 258.

[79] John Gibson of Adams County, *Debates*, II, 240, 241.

[80] See especially remarks of Mr. Howard, *Debates*, II, 203, 204.

[81] See remarks of Mr. Cassidy, *Debates*, II, 238-240; Mr. Biddle, *ibid.*, 246-248; Mr. Craig, *ibid.*, pp. 251-252; Mr. Temple, *ibid.*, 252-255; Mr. Cuyler, *ibid.*, p. 259. The *Philadelphia Public Ledger*, commenting on the position taken by the convention on this issue, found it surprising that "so intelligent a body as the Constitutional Convention should persist in the injustice of limited representation." In reply to the charge that without the limitation the state would be at the mercy of the large cities, the *Ledger* declared that past experience did not bear out this allegation. Indeed, the cities had been the great sufferers by state legislation, having imposed upon them an undue proportion of the taxes. Far from controlling the state, Philadelphia had had no United States Senator for thirty years and no governor for fifty years! The *Ledger*, March 6, 1873.

[82] Motion by Mr. Worrell, *Debates*, II, 248; the motion was rejected, *ibid.*; a motion to reconsider was adopted, *ibid.*, p. 251, and debate broke out anew. The motion was again rejected by a vote of 49 to 37, *ibid.*, p. 266.

tion, the provision reads: "No city or county shall be entitled to separate representation exceeding one-sixth of the whole number of Senators."[83]

Debate over representation in the House was not as bitter or as prolonged. There was discussion of the question of retention of the provision that each county should have at least one representative. Rural district delegates generally insisted upon this, though the inequities of the scheme were pointed out. There were other provisions in the formula which favored the rural areas. Counties with not more than four full quotas were assigned an additional representative for a fractional remainder of more than one-half, but those with more than four full quotas receive an additional representative only when the fractional remainder exceeds four-fifths of a ratio.[84]

The issue of single member districts also was discussed, and there were several delegates who advocated larger districts with representatives chosen by cumulative voting or some other plan of proportional representation. In the end the idea of proportional representation was not applied to the legislature, but neither was the single member district system imposed. The legislature was given discretion in the establishment of districts, which are supposed to be represented according to population. Districts may elect from one to four representatives, depending upon population size. A city or county with more than four representatives must be districted, so that no district will be assigned more than four.[85]

Executive Article

You may surround the Executive with threatened pains and penalties, trammel him with restraints and restrictions on his legitimate and necessary powers; nay, you may create armies, if you please, to see that the people are protected in their just rights and to compel the Executive of the State to perform his duties, and to restrain him from violating and exceeding his duties, and yet we come down, after all, to the plain, practical fact that in our form of government, and indeed in every government upon earth, you must trust men. If the men you place in power abuse their trust, our form of government provides the means of getting rid of them.

GOVERNOR ANDREW CURTIN[86]

It is interesting to note that the executive branch, with which the

---

[83]Art. II, Sec. 16.
[84]Art. II, Sec. 17. For debate of this issue see *Debates*, II, 266-318.
[85]Sec. 17.
[86]*Debates*, II, 369.

proponents of revision in 1837 were so much concerned, received scant attention in the debates of the 1872-73 convention. There were, however, some significant changes in the Executive Article. The term of office of the governor was increased from three to four years, but he was made ineligible to succeed himself in office.[87] The office of lieutenant-governor, which Thaddeus Stevens had proposed at the 1838 convention, was created.[88] The superintendent of public instruction replaced the supervisor of common schools[89] and the secretary of internal affairs was substituted for the surveyor general,[90] though the new officer, it was anticipated, would have broader functions. Fortunately the convention did not follow the prevailing pattern of state action of the day and hamper the subsequent growth of administrative power of the governor by constitutional dispersion of executive power. The Executive Article provided that executive power should be vested in the governor. It is true that not only the lieutenant-governor, but also the auditor-general, the treasurer, and the secretary of internal affairs were made elective; but, significantly, the secretary of the commonwealth, the attorney-general and the superintendent of public instruction were made appointive.[91]

The legislative powers of the governor were strengthened. The vote required to pass a bill over his veto was increased from two-thirds of those present and voting to two-thirds of all members elected to each house.[92] He was given the item veto of appropriation bills.[93] As a companion provision to the shift to biennial sessions, the governor was given not only the power to call special sessions[94] but also to name the legislative subjects upon which such a special session could act.[95]

Perhaps it was prestige of former Governor Curtin, who served as chairman of the Committee on the Executive, which gave the report such ready acceptance in the convention. The changes proposed by the committee were accepted with practically no debate save for the

---

[87] Art. IV, Sec. 3.

[88] Art. IV, Sec. 4.

[89] Art. IV, Sec. 20.

[90] Art. IV, Sec. 19.

[91] Art. IV, Sec. 8 provides for the appointment by the governor with consent of the Senate of the last named officers; election of the lieutenant governor for a term of four years is provided for in Sec. 4; election of the Secretary of Internal Affairs, Auditor General and Treasurer is provided for in Sec. 21. The Lieutenant Governor, Auditor General, and Treasurer were denied successive terms; the Auditor General was given a three year term and the Treasurer a two year term. Sec. 21.

[92] Art. IV, Sec. 15.

[93] Art. IV, Sec. 16.

[94] Art. IV, Sec. 12.

[95] Art. III, Sec. 25.

limitations placed on the pardoning power of the governor and the ineligibility of the governor to succeed himself in office.[96] Indeed, discussion of the entire Executive Article on first reading in the Committee of the Whole lasted only two days, and most of that time was devoted to discussion of the pardoning power.[97] Even the provision for ineligibility for succession provoked very limited debate. Charles R. Buckalew was the only delegate who spoke against the restriction, branding it as opposed to public interest. Why, he asked, should a governor who has proved himself to be a man of integrity and ability, who enjoys the confidence of the people, be denied a successive term? During the past quarter of a century, Pennsylvania had had several men who had filled the office with singular ability.[98]

On second reading Mr. Buckalew made a renewed attempt to eliminate the restriction. On a roll call vote, however, Buckalew's proposal mustered only seventeen aye votes.[99]

The primary concern of the delegates, as has been indicated, was with the limitation of the governor's power to grant pardons, and a variety of alternatives were discussed on the floor. One delegate even suggested that the pardoning board should be composed of all living ex-governors, but former Governor Curtin begged to be spared so harrowing a fate! He favored making the governor alone responsible for the exercise of executive clemency. In this position he was supported by Mr. Buckalew.

Finally the convention agreed to a board composed *ex officio* of two elective and two appointive officers: the lieutenant-governor, the secretary of internal affairs, the attorney general, and the secretary of the commonwealth. No pardon could be granted by the governor except upon approval by three of the four members of the pardon board.[100]

---

[96]There was some discussion of the provision for appointment of the Superintendent of Public Instruction, but this sprang from the fact that initially he was included on the pardoning board; when he was removed from the board, opposition to his appointment ended. *Debates*, II, 387.

[97]For discussion of the pardoning power, see *Debates*, II, 351-365; 367-384. In editorial comments, periodical literature, and discussion of the Constitution during the debates over ratification, the discussion of the nature of the executive branch or of the political role of the governor was wholly absent. Concern over the legislative branch seemed to absorb public interest to such a degree that the role of its partner in separation of powers evoked no public interest.

[98]*Debates*, II, 341-342. The section as reported by the Committee on Executive was agreed to in Committee of the Whole without revision, *ibid.*, p. 344.

[99]*Debates*, V, 205. Mr. MacVeagh and Mr. Woodward were included in the seventeen supporting Buckalew's proposals.

[100]Art. IV, Sec. 9. There had been severe criticism of the generous use of the par-

On second reading only a few inconsequential verbal changes were made,[101] and the Executive Article was approved on third reading with one minor change.[102]

Judiciary Article

The peculiar law in relation to the railway system, the railways themselves, the law relative to all corporations, the vast increase in the subjects of commercial law arising out of operations of these corporations, have precipitated new and entangling questions upon the courts which our fathers of the judiciary knew not of.... It is all new, and yet our courts stand still where they were forty years ago. It has seemed to me, sir, that everything in this world progresses except the judiciary system.   DAVID CRAIG[103]

The judiciary article was not subjected to radical change, though there were a number of modifications in the less basic aspects of the judicial system. The popular election of judges adopted in 1850 was continued.[104] The structure of the court system was only slightly modified. The register's court was abolished,[105] and the magistrates court substituted for the aldermanic court of Philadelphia.[106] There were some changes, also, in the structure of the common pleas court in Philadelphia and Allegheny counties.[107] The number of Supreme Court judges was increased from five to seven. Their tenure was increased from fifteen to twenty-one years, but Supreme Court judges were de-

---

doning power by Governor Geary. Democrats charged that prisoners had been released to swell the Republican vote in the presidential election of 1872. The *Pittsburgh Post* (Democratic), in commenting on abuses of the pardoning power declared: "Of late this power has been exercised with so free a hand, that lawyers of influence have no hesitation in bargaining for fees contingent upon obtaining pardons for convicted clients; the administration of the criminal law is becoming more and more a farce, and has in some measure become a net in which only the little fish are caught, while the big ones contrive to break through the meshes." November 26, 1872.

[101] Second reading occupied part of two consecutive days. *Debates*, V, 203-240.

[102] One section was added authorizing the Governor to call special sessions of the Senate to transact executive business, *ibid.*, VII, 444. The final action on the third reading appears at p. 444, and final approval of the report of the committee on Revision and Adjustment, VIII, 427.

[103] *Debates*, III, 708.

[104] Art. V, Sec. 2 and 15.

[105] Art. V, Sec. 1 formerly included the register's court. Art. V, Sec. 22 expressly abolishes the court.

[106] Art. V, Sec. 12.

[107] Provision was made for separate common pleas courts of co-ordinate jurisdiction. In Philadelphia there were to be four, and in Allegheny County two courts with three judges each. Art. V, Sec. 6.

clared ineligible for re-election. The limited vote plan, advocated by Charles R. Buckalew, was adopted for the choice of these judges when two or more were to be chosen.[108] The nisi prius jurisdiction of the court, the subject of widespread criticism, was abolished. Aside from a narrowly limited original jurisdiction for the purpose of the issuance of certain writs directed to state officers, the court was restricted to appellate jurisdiction, either on writ of error or writ of certiorari, as regulated by law.[109]

There were some changes in the provisions regarding judicial districts. Counties with a population of 40,000 or more inhabitants were constituted as separate judicial districts. Those with a smaller population were to be combined with other small counties to compose a district, or to be attached to a contiguous county large enough to be a separate district. No more than four counties could be included in any one district. The office of associate judge was abolished in the counties constituted separate districts, but retained for the combined districts.[110] Counties with a population in excess of 150,000 were assigned an orphan's court separate from common pleas.[111]

Though the jury system in its traditional form was retained, voluntary waiver of jury trial in civil cases was authorized.[112]

Though the judiciary article was not subjected to a major overhauling, it was nonetheless the subject of heated and, sometimes, acrimonious debate. On no issue did so intense a feeling of bitterness persist down to the last vote as between the majority which accepted and the minority which refused to accept the provisions finally adopted in Article V. Indeed, this feeling was carried over into the battle between those supporting and those opposing ratification.

Perhaps this sharp division of opinion should have been anticipated when the roll of delegates included 103 lawyers, several of whom had had considerable experience on the bench! The Committee on Judiciary, itself, had been unable to agree upon certain important provisions. The extent of the rift was soon revealed when the judiciary report was presented in Committee of the Whole.[113] In vain did the chairman of the

---

[108] Whenever two judges are to be chosen each voter casts one vote; when three are to be chosen each voter may vote for but two. This insures a two-party bench.

[109] Art. V, Sec. 3.

[110] Art. V, Secs. 4 and 5. The Constitution of 1838 had provided that not more than five counties could be included in a combined district.

[111] Art. V, Sec. 22.

[112] Art. I, Sec. 6; Art. V, Sec. 27.

[113] The Report of the Committee on Judiciary was presented by its chairman, Wil-

Committee on Judiciary, William H. Armstrong, plead with the dissenting members to wait until the complete plan was before the convention, so that the proposed judicial system could be seen as a whole, and the various provisions judged as a part of that whole.[114] The reading clerk had scarcely read the last word of Section 1 of the judiciary article as reported by the committee before its critics unleashed their bitter attack.

The primary issue at stake at this point in the debate was whether a "circuit court" should be included in the enumerated list of courts.[115] The three major positions expressed in the debate were represented in the thinking of the committee. The majority of the committee wished to create an intermediate appellate court, which they termed a circuit court, with its own bench of judges elected at large. This court would have both original and appellate jurisdiction. Judge Woodward and his supporters preferred an alternative scheme. The remaining five members of the committee were opposed to any form of a circuit court.

Mr. Armstrong, defending the position of the committee, pointed to the ever-mounting backlog of cases in the Supreme Court. The percentage of cases undisposed of at the end of each term was increasing at an alarming rate, and would probably reach 50 per cent by the end of 1873. In the western district, he declared, the whole term for 1873 would be spent in trying *ramenets;* all new cases would have to go over to the next term. This critical situation was not attributable to any inefficiency on the part of the court. In efficiency and independence the Pennsylvania court compared favorably with any other court in the land. The court was simply overburdened with cases. All members of the committee were agreed that some form of relief was "imperatively urgent," but the committee was not in full accord on the form it should take.

The majority report proposed the creation of a circuit court independent of all other courts, with its own judges. In cases involving less

---

liam H. Armstrong on March 27, 1873, *Debates*, III, 182-188. At this time three members of the committee filed dissenting reports disapproving in part the majority proposals, and two others gave notice they would file such reports later. For the minority reports see *ibid.*, pp. 189-191 for Daniel Kaine's dissenting report; pp. 191 for Samuel L. Purviance's and James L. Reynolds' reports. George Woodward and John M. Broomall gave notice of dissent.

[114]*Debates*, III, 639.

[115]The new section differed from the 1838 provision by adding a "circuit court" and deleting the "register's court."

than $500 the decision of the circuit court would be final. This would considerably lessen the volume of appeals coming before the Supreme Court. The highest tribunal, therefore, would have more time to hear and to consider the cases appealed to it. Larger cases, perhaps those above $2,000, would go directly to the Supreme Court, thus avoiding the delay of two appeals.[116]

Such a change in the court system not only would relieve the injustices resulting from the backlog in the hearing of appeals, it should also, Mr. Armstrong stated, improve the quality of decisions. In recent years the reversal of one case after another had become such a common practice that the court had found it necessary to index the cases considered overruled.

Judge Woodward, though accepting the idea of an intermediate appellate tribunal, disagreed with Mr. Armstrong at almost every other point. He suggested as an alternative to the committee plan the division of the state into twelve circuits, in each of which there would be a circuit court. A circuit court judge would be chosen in each district. He, sitting with two common pleas judges from the districts included in the circuit, would review the decisions appealed from the trial courts. The right of appeal to the Supreme Court would be preserved in all cases. He anticipated that the fairness of the review offered at this level would tend to discourage appeals, except when justified. The Supreme Court's burden would thus be lightened, but cases involving significant legal issues could reach the supreme tribunal whatever the amount involved in the controversy.[117] Opponents of this scheme insisted that twelve separate review courts would result in diversity of law throughout the state, and that the inclusion of common pleas judges on the bench would not give the full unprejudiced review that was desirable. Several variations of this scheme were offered and discussed at length.[118]

A third point of view expressed in the committee and on the convention floor was that no intermediate court was desired by the public, that none was necessary. One prominent member of the bar suggested that if the Supreme Court would mend its ways it could handle all the cases coming before it without undue delay. If the judges would sit

---

[116]*Debates*, III, 639-653. The proposed final jurisdiction of $500 was attacked by many delegates as creating a distinction between the rights of the poor and the rich. Mr. Gowen, *Debates*, III, 674-6; Mr. Baer, *ibid.*, pp. 717-719; Mr. Mitchell, *ibid.*, pp. 719-720; Mr. Meredith, *ibid.*, pp. 720-721.

[117]*Ibid.*, III, 653-663.

[118]*Ibid.*, III, 664-729.

longer, write shorter opinions, and use more discretion and judgment the backlogs would disappear. The tendency of judges to write long opinions, including remarks on related subjects not essential to the decision of the case at hand; the tendency to overrule old cases that do not agree precisely with the judges opinion, thus unsettling titles previously held good; a carelessness in decision-making, resulting in diametrically opposite opinions in the same volume of decisions—in these and similar practices could be found the cause of delays and the mountainous growth of litigation. Once a backlog had been established it was itself a cause of further appeals. Lawyers seeking a delay for their clients would take an appeal for the sole purpose of delay, irrespective of the merits of their cases. Let the Supreme Court mend its ways, and the pressure of cases would relax.[119]

There were also proposals for enlarging the size of the bench. With an enlarged bench the court could sit in divisions, or assign some of the judges the task of writing the opinions while their judicial brethren heard cases. It was generally agreed that the abolition of the nisi prius jurisdiction would be beneficial in freeing the court to perform its appellate duties.

After two days of debate the circuit court proposal was rejected by a vote of 62 to 22. Section 1 was approved as it had been under the 1838 constitution, except for the omission of the register's court and the district court.[120]

The second issue over which the convention divided sharply was the method of choosing judges. The committee proposed that judges of the Supreme Court should be appointed by the governor with the consent of the Senate, but that popular election should be retained for common pleas and other local judges. This, Mr. Armstrong explained, represented a workable compromise between the proponents of the two systems, a compromise for which popular support might be anticipated. The public was not likely to accept a complete reversal of the reform of 1850. The election of local judges, he granted, could be justified, since the voters would know the candidates and could intelligently pass judgment upon their qualifications. The popular election of Supreme Court judges, however, was fraught with many pitfalls. Candidates would be nominated by the political nominating conven-

---

[119]John M. Broomall, *ibid.*, III, 677-681.

[120]*Ibid.*, p. 728, f. Mr. Mann pointed out that the legislature had full power to create an intermediate court if the people found it desirable, *ibid.*, pp. 703-705. A similar position was taken by Daniel Kaine, who supported the idea of having the Court sit in divisions, *ibid.*, pp. 666, 667.

tions, which would consider the choice of judicial candidates from the point of view of their contribution to the success of the governor and his ticket. This generally would mean the choice of candidates who would aid in the geographical balancing of the state ticket. Judges would be voted in and out of office according to the political fortunes of the party ticket. Far wiser than this would be the appointment of judges with the consent of two-thirds of the Senate. The extraordinary majority required would make the support of some members of the opposition indispensable, and hence promote a nonpartisan spirit in appointments. The committee felt, furthermore, that appointment would provide a greater safeguard against undue influence by large corporate interests, since political conventions were more susceptible to corporate influence than the governor and Senate.[121]

Judge Woodward, who was insistent throughout the whole controversy over the judiciary article that his own plan should be substituted for that of the committee,[122] immediately proposed an amendment providing for the appointment of all judges.[123] Though at the 1836 convention he had fought for limited tenure for judges to make them at least in some degree amenable to popular will, he now argued for their appointment. Popular election of judges along with other public officers he thought unwise. The people were not in a position to judge the attainments and qualifications of judicial candidates. Under the elective system a judge must be a politician to win.

For the past twenty-two years, he pointed out, Pennsylvania had had the elective system. He had served on the bench under both systems and had seen the workings of both. Experience had convinced him that the old system was better. As a general rule the men whom the politicians controlling the nominating conventions would be least likely to choose would make the best judges.[124]

On this issue the Philadelphia delegation was split. Only two of his fellow Philadelphians supported his position in debate. They, however, gave a spirited defense of the principle of appointment, charging that experience in Philadelphia had demonstrated the fallacy of the elective system. Judges in Philadelphia—and the experience in New

---

[121]*Debates*, IV, 28-33.

[122]Mr. Woodward always referred to the Committee draft as Mr. Armstrong's plan, inferring that it did not represent the thinking of the Committee.

[123]His proposal was a substitute Section 2, which included other matters as well, *Debates*, III, 732.

[124]*Debates*, III, 733-38; 742-745.

York City had been the same—were chosen by a score of "pot-house" politicians. It was an admitted fact "that no man in the city of Philadelphia could be elected as a judge no matter what his antecedents might be," against the opposition of the men "who understood the manipulation of party politics and the control of primary elections." Appointment was superior to election for judges because an office is best filled where the sense of responsibility is greatest not only in him who holds office, but in him who appoints. Where, asked one of the defenders of appointment, is the responsibility in the people? Who feels to blame if the man for whom he has voted proves bad? When one person is vested with the power of appointment the sense of responsibility is fastened upon him. Furthermore, the people in choosing judges generally are controlled by the political excitement involved in the contests for political offices taking place at the same election. The judge elected in such a political contest feels beholden to the politicians who nominated and elected him. Independence of the judiciary could best be achieved by appointment, preferably for life tenure.[125]

Wayne MacVeagh, regarded by his contemporaries as an outstanding member of the Pennsylvania bar, also defended Judge Woodward's proposal. He urged adoption of the appointive system primarily on the grounds that a court is not a representative body of the people and should not "represent any interest, any party or any combination whatever." The judiciary, he declared, is degraded by being made a political department. Candidates nominated by a partisan political convention ought to serve in a political office and ought to represent the viewpoint of the people who elected them to office. A judge necessarily cannot do this. All writers upon the subject, from Aristotle to John Stuart Mill, had advocated the training of an exclusive profession for the administration of justice. Any proposal to submit to the ordeal of political selection a separate and trained profession set apart for the work of judges would do an injustice to one's intelligence. This would be true even if elections were pure and undefiled. "In the present era of economic development," he asserted, it was "indispensable to have a judiciary independent beyond reproach and without fear." The choice presented to the convention was whether the judges should be appointed by a responsible authority or by the "irresponsible authority of a partisan caucus and subsequent nominating convention." In either case partisanship would be involved, but the governor has his own self-respect and reputation to preserve.[126]

---

[125]Mr. Temple, *Debates*, III, 751-761; Mr. Gowen, *ibid.*, pp. 772-778.
[126]*Debates*, III, 761-765.

The proponents of appointment were outnumbered, both in debate and on vote, by the advocates of election. Even the compromise proposed by the committee was unacceptable to them. In its place they adopted an amendment providing for popular election of all judges. John N. Purviance, who gave the leading speech in defense of this proposal, asserted that the people were the safest depository of power. Under the elective system the judges had been at least the equal if not better than the appointive judges who had preceded them. The real reason why the amendment of 1850 had been adopted was the one-sided nature of the judiciary. Inevitably appointment by the governor meant a partisan appointment. When one party was in control of the executive branch for a long period of time a one-party bench was the product.[127]

More than a dozen delegates rose to support this substitute proposal. They pointed to the high quality of judges then serving on the bench and denied that popular election was any more subject to base political influences than political appointment. Indeed, they argued, the system of appointment was subject to all the weaknesses alleged against the elective system. If the people were competent to choose a pure governor who would choose judges wisely, why were they not competent also to choose good judges? They further insisted that popular election was the best method of maintaining the courts as a coordinate branch under separation of powers.[128]

On second reading of the judiciary article, Judge Woodward renewed his proposal for appointment of judges, but his motion to amend Section 2 was rejected by a vote of 54 to 18.[129]

Although the proposal was never debated on the floor of the convention, a resolution was introduced and referred to the Committee on the Judiciary which provided for a system of appointment of judges by the governor and a subsequent popular vote upon appointees, a plan somewhat similar in basic thought to the "Pennsylvania Plan." This

---

[127]*Debates*, IV, 4-6. Mr. Samuel A. Purviance had introduced an amendment providing for the election of Supreme Court judges by districts; he withdrew his amendment to permit introduction by his colleague, Thomas MacConnell (of Allegheny County) of a general proposal for popular election of all judges, *ibid.*, III, 729; 754. The amendment of Mr. MacConnell was adopted in Committee of the Whole, *ibid.*, IV, 41.

[128]See remarks of Messrs. Dallas, Darlington, Horton, Sharpe, Ewing, Worrell, H. G. Smith, Bowman, Broomall, H. W. Palmer, Landis, Howard, and Simpson, *Debates*, III, 745-750; 750-753; 766, 767; 767-772; IV, 6-11; 12, 13; 14-17; 17-20; 20; 20-22; 22-25; 35-36; 39-41.

[129]*Debates*, V, 240. On this vote the Philadelphia delegation split 10 to 4 against the proposal.

antedated the Cleveland Bar Association proposal by half a century, and the California Plan by sixty years.[130]

There was a lively debate over practically every section of the Judiciary Article. Debate wore on through tedious details as each lawyer espoused or opposed proposals, basing his arguments upon his personal experience as a practicing lawyer or judge, citing cases as varied as the differing interests of the state. As if this were not enough, horrible examples were invoked from the experience of neighboring states. Differences were especially sharp regarding the size of judicial districts, the abolition or retention of the office of associate judge, and the special provisions for Allegheny and Philadelphia counties establishing multiple common pleas courts. On the latter issue the Philadelphia delegation was irreconcilably split, and debate at times degenerated into bitter personal exchanges between Philadelphia delegates. No wonder it took five weeks to hammer out the twenty-seven sections of the Judiciary Article! Second reading consumed an additional fifteen days. The final approval on third reading on October 9 came only after defeat of renewed proposals to abolish associate judgeships, to eliminate the limited vote in choice of Supreme Court judges, and to modify the provisions regarding the common pleas in Philadelphia.

Unreconciled, the opponents of the article demanded that it should be separately submitted for ratification, but this proposal was rejected by the convention. They then presented a petition signed by forty-six members.[131] This they pointed out was equal to more than one-third of the membership as required by the Act of 1872 under which the convention had been called. The rejection of their proposal intensified the tone of bitterness so frequently displayed in debate on this article.[132]

---

[130]Introduced by Mr. Barclay. The proposal applied to all judges other than Supreme Court judges. The Governor would appoint, and the appointee named would then be submitted at the next general election. If approved, the appointee would have a ten year term; if rejected, the Governor would appoint another, subject to the same provision. *Debates*, I, 113.

[131]Presented by Mr. Lamberton, *Debates*, VIII, 682.

[132]When the proposal was made, after approval on third reading, that the Judiciary Article should be submitted separately, Charles R. Buckalew took the floor to deny the applicability of the provision of the Act of 1872. Acknowledging that he was the author of the provision, Mr. Buckalew explained that the law provided for two alternative forms of action. The convention might either propose a revised constitution or propose amendments to the constitution. In the latter case the separate submission of amendments could be compelled by the request of one-third of the members. In event a new constitution was drafted (as had been done), it could not be torn apart and submitted in a dismembered form. *Debates*, VIII, 567, 568. The convention sustained Mr. Buckalew's position. When Mr. Lamberton brought in

his petition, *ibid.*, p. 682, Mr. Armstrong challenged its acceptance by the convention. Some members who had signed the document were not present; furthermore, the legislature had no right to so limit the convention after its authorization. Nevertheless, Mr. Lamberton pressed consideration of a resolution for the ordering of a separate submission as required by the petition. This was rejected by a vote of 49 to 44, *ibid.*, p. 695. The convention also rejected by 63 to 38 a proposal that there should be a separate vote on all provisions for which a petition of one-third of the members should be submitted to the president of the convention.

CHAPTER 7: CHAINS FOR THE GIANTS: POLITICAL MACHINES, CORPORATIONS, RAILROADS

Suffrage and Elections

As the country becomes denser in population, as wealth accumulates, as the various interests of society become more diverse, its affairs more complicated and dependent upon legislation, this evil of electoral corruption must increase and swell in volume. You must correct the arrangements for elections in order to check it. Cumulative voting will check it.... Then illegitimate, pernicious and selfish interests in a State will not use the machinery of your electoral system for the purpose of poisoning the sources of political power, because there will not be a sufficient motive.

CHARLES R. BUCKALEW[1]

NEXT to the problems springing out of legislative corruption, the convention was concerned with the elimination of election irregularities. The Democrats and liberal Republicans were much concerned with the necessity for such reform. They generally charged that the registry law of Philadelphia was used to exclude both Democrats and liberal Republicans from voting, and that Philadelphia election officials revised election returns to provide whatever majority was necessary to produce state victories and to keep corrupt officials in control in Philadelphia. The motivation for such corruption was deeply rooted in the fee system for compensation of county "row" officers. The methods used were

---

[1]From a speech before the United States Senate on behalf of cumulative voting, published in *Buckalew on Proportional Representation*, Philadelphia (1872), p. 21.

legion. There were charges of "colonization"; ballot-box stuffing; irregularities in the form of farcical naturalization proceedings on a wholesale scale by which hundreds of aliens acquired a doubtful citizenship to qualify them for voting; and especially the "counting in" of the right candidates and the "counting out" of opponents, irrespective of actual vote of the electorate. In state-wide elections, Philadelphia returns usually were held up until the returns from the rest of the state had been reported, so that Philadelphia election officials could correctly tailor the Philadelphia vote to produce radical Republican victory.[2]

While the convention was in session, Senator A. K. McClure, liberal Republican, made a dramatic appeal before the state Senate for reform action by that assembly. In the course of his speech he graphically portrayed the methods used by the local registry officials. The election canvassers, he declared, practically had the authority to disfranchise whom they chose. The "power to disfranchise any citizen," he asserted, "is absolute, even beyond the power of the courts." He then related the difficulty he had had in getting his own name on the registry list. The canvassers and election officials in Philadelphia he characterized as "disreputable," some of them "utterly desperate and chauvanistic men" who made use of "convicts, professional bullies and repeaters" in carrying out their fraudulent schemes. He urged the repeal of the existing registry law, and the establishment of a new registration system to be administered by a bipartisan commission rather than by the board of aldermen of Philadelphia.[3]

In the convention itself consideration of election reforms and suffrage aroused a lively debate which lasted for five weeks. The remedies proposed for the correction of election evils were twofold. Reform leaders from Philadelphia, and Democrats generally, proposed as the first remedy that the election ballots should be numbered by election officials and the number recorded beside the name of the voter on the ballot list. As further protection they proposed that the voter should be required to endorse his name on the ballot. This proposal provoked a sharp division of opinion, though it had received the endorsement of the Committee on Suffrage, Election, and Representation.[4]

---

[2]Democrats charged that they had been deprived of victory by such methods in the 1866 election of the governor, when Philadelphia returned the necessary 4,500 vote majority for Geary's election by that slim margin.

[3]Speech reported verbatim in the *Pittsburgh Post*, March 10, 1873. He pointed out that Philadelphia, with a population of 300,000 less than New York, had 20,000 more names on the voting list, "a palpable, indisputable fraud."

[4]*Debates*, I, 503.

Some Democrats, aroused by the enormity of election scandals, would have gladly substituted viva-voce voting for the ballot.[5] They recognized, however, that such a proposal could not command a majority in the convention. They, therefore, joined their party members in advocating the numbering and signing of ballots. This, reform advocates insisted, would not destroy the secrecy of the ballot. For one thing, there was no secrecy to destroy, for each party printed its ballot on a different type of paper. Members of the election board could readily, and did, keep track of how the vote was running, and party officials could tell how anyone voted. Under the proposed system the election officials would be sworn to secrecy, so that privacy would be preserved! The primary advantage gained would be that in election contests involving fraud, the voter could identify his ballot in court and thus prove that his ballot had been tampered with or incorrectly tallied. There would be a further advantage; the voter, knowing that his ballot could be identified, would vote more thoughtfully.[6] Thus, Charles R. Buckalew, leading Democratic spokesman, endorsed the plan even though he defended secrecy of the ballot as essential. He regarded the numbering and signing of ballots as the only available means of stopping the election frauds. "The party that obtains the corruptible vote," he declared, "sweeps the board in the great game of politics, and so long as the system is permitted to remain unchanged it will produce its degrading and detestable fruits."[7]

The Democrats were united and insistent upon their reform, but there were other voices raised in the convention which opposed this

---

[5] Judge Woodward insisted that there was no necessity for voting secrecy in the United States where the tenant-landlord situation, which had made secrecy in voting essential in England, was absent. Secrecy of the ballot in Pennsylvania had been responsible for the production of serious abuses. "If a man has an opinion to express upon a public question, let him come up and express it like a man." Pennsylvanians, he declared, do not hesitate about expressing their opinions, why should they have to "sneak up and deposit a secret ballot?" Viva-voce voting would go far toward eliminating the frauds in Philadelphia. *Debates*, I, 726-29. J. Alexander Simpson voiced similar ideas, *ibid.*, pp. 729-31; as did former Governor Curtin, *ibid.*, pp. 741-43; and Franklin Gowen, *ibid.*, pp. 778-82. Woodward and Simpson were from Philadelphia.

[6] See remarks of Joseph G. Patton, *Debates*, I, 740-41; William Lilly, *ibid.*, pp. 741-43; J. P. Wetherill, *ibid.*, pp. 747-48; Thomas Howard, *ibid.*, pp. 749-50; John R. Read, *ibid.*, pp. 750-51; Robert A. Lamberton, *ibid.*, pp. 752-53; Lewis C. Cassidy, *ibid.*, pp. 775-77. Wetherill, Read and Cassidy were from Philadelphia. Ballots generally were printed by the political parties and the voter could get them at headquarters; in addition the partisan press usually obligingly printed ballots that could be clipped from the newspaper and used. Indeed, a person could write his own ballot.

[7] *Debates*, I, 731-33.

proposal with equal vigor. Opposition came in part from Philadelphia Republicans, whose speeches minimized alleged abuses, but was especially strong from delegates representing interior and western counties.

The position of the Philadelphia Republicans was made clear as delegate after delegate arose to denounce the plan already endorsed by Philadelphia reformers.[8] The clash between the two factions became sufficiently sharp so that some delegates testily complained that the delegation from the Quaker City thought that the convention had been called to settle their local problems, rather than to consider the interests of the state as a whole.

Opponents of the ballot plan declared that the scheme, far from purifying elections, would demoralize the people, and place in the hands of the politicians a whip by which they could compel party members to stay in line. It would, indeed, give to the vote manipulator an excellent device for his own purposes. "The very class imposed upon in these frauds," warned one delegate, "are the ones who will have to go to some one who can write to sign their names. This provision would make it possible for corrupt politicians to go around ahead of time and secure these men before the hurly-burly of election day," sign their ballots for them, and pay them for their votes.[9]

Many delegates expressed fear of the dangers involved in the impairment of ballot secrecy. A delegate from the anthracite coal area, for example, denounced the scheme as playing into the hands of corporate interests, which undoubtedly would attempt to consolidate their economic power by seizing political power. Since most men would in the future find employment with corporations, it would be dangerous to set up a system under which the employer could tell how his employees had voted.[10]

There were many others who joined in this expression of fear and clung to secrecy of the ballot as the best guarantee of an uncontrolled vote in elections. They came from all sections of the state.[11] Delegates from the rural counties were particularly sensitive to the implications of the provision. They complained that those who could not write would

---

[8] E. C. Knight, George Biddle, Samuel Wherry and James Newlin, delegates from Philadelphia spoke against the proposal, *Debates*, I, 723, 724; 764, 765; 771; 790.

[9] Thomas Struthers of Warren County, *Debates*, II, 22-24.

[10] Lin Bartholomew of Schuylkill County, *Debates*, I, 753-756.

[11] William J. Baer of Somerset, *Debates*, I, 718-719; Morton F. Elliott of Tioga, *ibid.*, I, 720-22; D. W. Patterson and J. W. F. White of Allegheny, *ibid.*, pp. 722, 723; 762, 763; John Collins, *ibid.*, p. 789; Samuel A. Wherry of Philadelphia, *ibid.*, p. 790.

be discouraged from voting. Illiteracy was significantly higher in the rural areas than in the cities, so that such a provision would work more hardship in the country districts. Why should the people in the country be penalized for the sins of Philadelphia? If such a caustic remedy was necessary there, restrict the remedy to the area where it was needed![12] Wayne MacVeagh, leader of the Republicans, declared that the whole northern tier of counties was opposed to the proposal.[13]

One city delegate, despairing of the efficacy of any legislative or constitutional reforms on this issue, declared that the remedy proposed would not cure the disease. The fault lay, he pointed out, not with the law, but with the people themselves. There were already sufficient laws on the statute book to prevent fraud. If the people in sufficient numbers were really interested there would be no fraud. The "good" people were too busy with their own affairs—the well-to-do acquiring more wealth, and the rest pursuing a livelihood—to be concerned with public affairs. Consequently those who were willing to devote their entire time and thought to politics controlled affairs. The only real remedy would be a broad popular interest.[14]

Another delegate pointed to the fact that England had recently adopted a ballot reform that Pennsylvania might later want to adopt. The government would henceforth print uniform ballots with the names of all candidates of all parties on the same ballot. The legislature of Pennsylvania should not be barred from providing for such a system if it worked well in England. Details in the constitution, as here proposed, would tie the hands of the legislature.[15]

After five days of debate the proposal was rejected by a vote of 39 to 57.[16]

This, however, was but a temporary setback. The next day a motion for reconsideration was introduced, and arguments were renewed. Mr. Buckalew urged a speedy ending of the debate pointing out that the issue had been thoroughly examined in exhaustive debate. To this suggestion, Mr. MacVeagh replied caustically, objecting to the reconsideration of a defeated provision at a time when several men well-known to be opposed to it were absent. He hinted that the Democrats had decided to force reconsideration, cut off debate, and rush

---

[12] Daniel C. Kaine of Fayette County, *Debates*, I, 768.
[13] *Debates*, II, 89; Mr. Carter stated that there was strong opposition in Delaware, Chester and Berks, especially among the Germans, *ibid.*, pp. 92, 93.
[14] James W. M. Newlin of Philadelphia, *Debates*, I, 771.
[15] Samuel Minor of Crawford County, *Debates*, I, 769-771.
[16] *Debates*, II, 29.

through action while they had a temporary majority. This was one of the few instances when party differences clashed openly on the floor.[17]

After heated and somewhat bitter exchanges between the opposing delegates,[18] the former vote was reversed by a vote of 53 to 47.[19] As finally written into the constitution this section made the signing of the ballot optional, though the numbering of ballots and the recording of the number beside the name of the voter on the official ballot list was made mandatory.[20]

The second method proposed by the committee to remedy election evils was a change in the date of elections. The October state election should be changed to correspond with the national election date in November. This the committee members explained would reduce the practice of importing repeaters from other states, since the national election in surrounding states would fall on the same day. They also proposed the holding of all local elections throughout the state on the same day, the third Tuesday of March. The suggested change in the general election was agreed to after some discussion,[21] but there were differences of opinion expressed regarding the advisability of a separate spring election, and indeed the advisability of requiring all municipal elections to fall on the same day.[22] Most delegates from Philadelphia supported the proposal, though it was objected to by many of the rural and small city delegates. After much discussion the proposal was modified and accepted. The third Tuesday in February was agreed upon as the date for municipal elections.[23]

The only important change in suffrage qualifications was the removal of the color restriction which had been written into the 1838 constitution, but which was now prohibited by the recently adopted Fifteenth Amendment to the national Constitution. There were a few

---

[17]The motion for reconsideration was introduced by Mr. Hunsicker, *Debates*, II, 87; Mr. Buckalew's remarks, *ibid.*, p. 95; Mr. MacVeagh's comments, *ibid.*, p. 95.

[18]The clash between Mr. MacVeagh and Mr. Gowen was especially bitter.

[19]*Debates*, II, 124. The division was largely on party lines, the Democrats voting for the reform, and Republicans against. There were a few Republicans who joined the Democrats including Mr. McAllister, chairman of the committee. The *Pittsburgh Commercial* declared that the renegade Republicans should be politically ostracized by their party.

[20]Art. VIII, Sec. 4.

[21]*Debates*, I, 228.

[22]Hugh N. McAllister, chairman, defended the principle of a common date to prevent importing of repeaters, *Debates*, I, 241.

[23]Art. VIII, Sec. 3.

verbal changes, and some safeguards were added to correct abuses that had grown up. Thus, the requirement of at least one month's citizenship to qualify was added to discourage the frequent abuses in naturalization proceedings at the behest of election manipulators; the substitution of a two-months residence in the voting district for the former ten-day requirement was intended to check colonization of close voting districts; and the requirement that the qualifying tax should have been assessed at least two months and paid at least one month before the election was inserted to reduce abuses in party payment of taxes for fraudulent voters.[24]

An unsuccessful attempt was made to remove the taxpaying qualification. This requirement was omitted from the committee draft. Its omission was defended by the committee chairman, Hugh N. McAllister. The committee had reached its decision, he said, on the basis of the principle that "the right of suffrage did not depend upon property, nor upon the payment of taxes, but that it belonged to man as a man and not because he was a taxpayer." The right of suffrage is a natural right in the sense of a social political right. It "is correllated with the right of property, but not dependent upon it; it cannot be taken away by the non-payment of a tax, for it is an absolute right." Many evils had developed in connection with the existing requirement of taxpaying. In some instances, taxes had not been assessed, and persons otherwise qualified had been barred from voting. Fraudulent schemes of political vote manipulators had been based upon the tax requirement. In some instances a tax of five cents a voter was assessed. Associating the suffrage with such a nominal sum belittled the suffrage.[25]

One prominent Philadelphian supporting McAllister's position, argued that "to be taxed, one must be represented, but to be represented, one need not necessarily to be taxed." He was of the opinion "that the right of suffrage should be as untrammeled as possible."[26] He and several other delegates stressed the fact that in actual practice the taxpaying qualification simply increased the control of the politicians, who paid the taxes for the voters. One Philadelphian stated that in Philadelphia the receiver of taxes issued hundreds of thousands of blank receipts to his political favorites for distribution to fraudulent voters. The party out of power simply printed its own and forged the name of the tax receiver. Both parties were guilty. Elimination of

---

[24]Constitution of 1838, Article III, Sec. 1; Constitution of 1874, Article VIII, Sec. 1.
[25]*Debates*, I, 632-645.
[26]Edward R. Worrell, *Debates*, I, 652.

the tax requirement thus would aid in reduction of election fraud.[27]

The proponents of the taxpaying qualification[28] defended it vigorously.

No story of the suffrage debate would be complete without some reference to woman suffrage. The proposal of woman suffrage was made early in the convention by John M. Broomall of Delaware County, who first introduced it as a proposal to be referred to the Committee on Suffrage, Election, and Representation,[29] and later renewed it in Committee of the Whole[30] as an amendment to the majority report.

From the time Mr. Broomall proposed his amendment on February 4, until his withdrawal of it late in the afternoon of February 7, the convention did little else than discuss the "loathsome"[31] amendment. The contest was conducted with a flourish of ornate oratory. Speeches were replete with gentlemanly obeisance to the virtue and nobility of women, qualified by condescending reference to the frivolous nature of these charming creatures with their beribboned fluttery bonnets. Remarks were gemmed with quotations from poetry and with citations from Scripture, which by doubtful logic were bent to support or deny women's claim to equality of political rights. Debate was weighted down with solemn discussion of natural law and natural rights, of conventional law and grave questions of expediency. It was lightened, also, by moments of humor. Thus, one delegate ribbingly painted the picture of the suffrage champions as variously employed preparing dinner, quieting the baby with paregoric, or singing lullabies to a sleepless infant, while their respective wives attended hustings, carried transparencies in political parades, or juggled figures of election returns to count in the right candidates! Mockingly, another delegate offered an "olive branch" substitute:[32]

Every male citizen of the age twenty-one, and all damsels and spinsters above the age of forty, or of doubtful age, citizens of the United States ... shall have the right of suffrage.

Unabashed by ridicule and torrents of oratory, Mr. Broomall refused to give ground. His opponents insisted that women would be

---

[27]*Debates*, I, 653, 654. H. G. Smith expressed a similar view, *ibid.*, p. 631.

[28]Amendment proposed by Jerome B. Niles, *Debates*, I, 629.

[29]*Debates*, I, 89.

[30]*Debates*, I, 525.

[31]So described by Judge George Woodward.

[32]Remarks of James Heverin, *Debates*, I, 622; "amendment" by James Boyd, *ibid.*, p. 609.

degraded by voting, that not only would the trains of their garments be trampled upon as they elbowed their way through rough crowds of rude, half-drunken men to reach the polls, but also that that refinement and high moral quality which men cherished in women would likewise be trampled and destroyed. Such arguments Mr. Broomall brushed aside. The devotion to women of men who took such a position he characterized as applying "simply to women of the gentlemen's own imagination—the painted butterflies who are supposed to be kept in costly glass cases, and watched by men for fear, if they should step outside, they will soil their wings." The remaining arguments of his opponents, he said, could be summed up in the words: "It never has been the law heretofore, and therefore it must not be hereafter."[33]

He denied that voting is a natural right, as argued by some of his opponents, but rather a conventional right to protect natural rights; and, he inquired of his opponents, how could they claim that women any less than men needed the suffrage to protect those rights? To him the claim that the husband as the head of the family cast the vote of the family seemed absurd. Why should half of the citizens be permitted to vote and not the other half? How could one say that men could truly represent the interests of the other half of the citizenry? Quoting Buckle, he insisted, "There is no class of citizens, and no single citizen, who can safely be entrusted with the permanent and exclusive possession of political power."[34]

Concluding his remarks, Mr. Broomall declared that those delegates who wished to continue man's tutelage over women and to hedge them around with legal disabilities lest they should not be sufficiently careful of their dignity, should limit their want of confidence to the women of their own constituencies. "The women with whom I associate are not of that character. They are women capable of being trusted wherever their good judgment directs them to go, and wherever they go you may be sure they will be surrounded by a halo of fairness, of right, of justice, of sobriety and equity, before which all that is corrupt and foul, and wrong will disappear."[35]

There were other bold champions of women's rights who joined Mr. Broomall,[36] but they were outnumbered by the redoubtable

---

[33]*Debates*, I, 647-48.
[34]*Debates*, I, 648; quotation from Buckle, p. 548.
[35]*Debates*, I, 649. The women suffragists applauded Mr. Broomall for his "chaste" remarks in defense of their cause.
[36]Messrs. Campbell, Darlington, Horton, Temple, and Wright.

champions of women's virtue.³⁷ It was not until Mr. Broomall, under pressure from a time-limitation for debate on the issue, withdrew his amendment that both sides sheathed their verbal swords and retired from the lists.³⁸ When the proposal was renewed on second reading,³⁹ it was defeated without further debate by a vote of 67 to 22.⁴⁰

Local Government

Nothing can so surely bring a Constitution into contempt as to find that it has usurped the province of the Legislature, or the province of the local governments of the cities, and hedged them round with such restrictions that, in one or two years, there will be a desire to break down the Constitution, in order to prevent its trammels from entirely disabling the people's representatives. This is only a general view; it applies particularly to the Legislature, but it applies with equal force to the councils of a great city like Philadelphia, or to a city like Pittsburgh, and even to the smaller municipal governments of boroughs or cities in the State.

FRANKLIN B. GOWEN⁴¹

A number of new provisions were written into the constitution in respect to local government. Thus, the legislature was barred from erecting any new county which would reduce an existing county to less than four hundred square miles or to fewer than 20,000 inhabitants; or which itself would contain a smaller area or population.⁴² There were some lively exchanges on the floor of the convention over this provision, and there were many who questioned whether such a severe stricture should be authorized. Some delegates opined that never again would a new county be created, though the rapid growth in population would justify it.⁴³ The strongest opposition came from Carbon and Luzerne

---

³⁷Besides Messrs. Boyd, Heverin and Woodward, already cited, Messrs. Alricks, Bartholomew, Gowen, Palmer, Stewart and Walker.

³⁸The debates are reported in full in *Debates*, I, 525-628. The convention received petitions almost daily from various parts of the state demanding adoption of woman suffrage.

³⁹The motion was made by Mr. Campbell and seconded by Mr. Broomall, *Debates*, V, 127.

⁴⁰*Debates*, V, 128.

⁴¹*Debates*, II, 701.

⁴²Article XIII.

⁴³*Debates*, III, 247-270. They were not far wrong in their prognostication; but one county has been created since 1874. The proposed provision was agreed to on first reading in Committee of the Whole, *ibid.*, III, 270; it was accepted in slightly amended form on second reading, *ibid.*, V, 406; approval on third reading as reported from the Committee on Revision and Adjustment is reported, *ibid.*, VII, 723.

counties. There was at that time a movement to create a new county out of part of Luzerne County, a movement which bore fruit in 1878 in the creation of Lackawanna County. Delegates from that section of Luzerne County were opposed to the constitutional limitation because they felt that their separation from the existing county would be rendered more difficult.

The real purpose of the article, however, was not to check any genuine movement for the division of a county to meet the needs of the people, but to eliminate abuses primarily by persons with speculative real estate schemes.[44] In this regard Judge Woodward declared, "I do not know of any greater source of iniquity and corruption in Pennsylvania."[45]

County governmental structure was frozen into the new constitution in considerable detail. The older constitutional offices[46] were continued. The county commissioners, treasurer, surveyor, and auditors or controller were added to the list.[47] All were made elective. Buckalew's limited vote plan was instituted for choice of county commissioners and county auditors.[48]

The fee system for compensation of county officers was abolished in counties containing over 150,000 inhabitants. Salaries were limited to not more than the aggregate amount of fees earned during the year.[49] This was especially significant in relation to Philadelphia, where several of the fee-paid officers reaped a fortune annually.[50]

By comparison, the Article on Cities and City Charters was very brief, containing but three short sections. Provision was made for the chartering of cities whenever a majority of the electors of a town or borough with a population of ten thousand or more should so vote at a general election.[51]

---

[44]While the convention was in session there was in progress in the legislature one such scheme, and there were rumors regarding the liberal expenditures being made by its promoter to press it through the legislature. The promoter of Minnequa County owned the land, which he believed would be improved in speculative value if the county were created. Significantly, there was no one living in the area concerned. *Pittsburgh Gazette*, March 21, 1873.

[45]*Debates*, VII, 346, 347.

[46]The sheriff, coroner, prothonotary, register of wills, recorder of deeds, clerk of courts, and district attorney were already constitutional offices.

[47]Article XIV, Sec. 1.

[48]Article XIV, Sec. 7.

[49]Article XIV, Sec. 5.

[50]See editorial "Salaries, Not Fees," *Philadelphia Public Ledger*, January 20, 1873.

[51]Article XV, Sec. 1.

Section 2 forbade the incurrence of debt or expenditures by a municipal commission, except pursuant to an appropriation by the municipal council. This prohibition was for the purpose of checking the practice which had grown up in the administration of city public works, parks, and similar projects. Interests defeated in the city council customarily appealed to Harrisburg and obtained a law providing for the locally rejected construction or development and for the administration of the project by a commission appointed by the legislature. Any expenditure or debt incurred would then be imposed upon the city without the necessity of authorization by city council. This abuse was a frequent occurrence in Philadelphia and Pittsburgh city affairs.[52]

The final section required municipalities to create sinking funds to amortize their funded debts. This article was kept brief, but it must be remembered that there were provisions in other articles that had a direct bearing on municipal affairs.

As already indicated in the discussion of legislative powers, the General Assembly was barred from granting municipal charters by special laws. This was regarded by the convention members as the most significant action in respect to city government. Important, also, were the provisions in the same section prohibiting the legislature from authorizing, laying out, or opening roads, streets, or alleys, or altering them once they were laid out. The action thus prohibited had been a constant source of irritation in Philadelphia.[53]

The aspect of local government which provoked the most discussion in the convention was local government finance. Particular attention was given to the mounting debt of local communities. This problem was especially acute in growing urban areas faced with the

---

[52]A Philadelphia delegate pointed to the evils of the system by two illustrations: A commission had been appointed by the legislature to build a bridge across the Schuylkill River at a cost of over a million dollars; though the city had no control over the expenditure, it must pay the bill. Similarly, another bridge was authorized at the behest of some passenger railway companies, though the city had refused their request. Commissions as used in these cases were "not responsible to anybody, neither the courts, councils nor the Legislature, but by mandamus upon the city treasury, they can compel the payment of all the indebtedness they incur." Mr. Bardsley of Philadelphia, *Debates* III, 117, ff. Mr. Ewing of Pittsburgh declared that his city had them also, and that their "fruit is evil, and only evil." *Ibid.*, p. 119.

[53]See editorial in *Philadelphia Public Ledger* entitled "Has the City Any Rights," discussing the control and management of streets in Philadelphia, appearing in the February 7, 1873 edition of the paper. The same paper carried an editorial on April 26, 1873, under the caption, "Before the Governor," in which it reported that there were at least a dozen bills on the governor's desk relating to streets in Philadelphia "vacating, altering lines, reducing widths, ordering or opening new streets."

necessity of undertaking public improvements.[54] After much discussion, they adopted the existing provision limiting debt to 7 per cent of the assessed valuation of taxable property.[55] They added, however, the requirement that sufficient tax must be assessed to meet interest charges and to amortize the debt within thirty years.[56]

The convention considered, but ultimately rejected, various proposals which would have crystallized in the constitution the structure of city government and have defined the powers of the mayor and council.[57] Those opposing the inclusion of such provisions pointed to the hazards of putting such details into the constitution. They suggested that with special legislation outlawed the legislature was a safe repository of the power to define the structure of city government and the duties of city officials.[58] In the end this opinion prevailed.[59]

Economic and Social Provisions

There is a general feeling in the public mind of distrust and suspicion and alarm at the growth and magnitude of the power of these corporations. It is believed that they control the legislation of the country, and the people of Pennsylvania have been looking to the convention with a confidence that they feel in no other public body for some protection against real or imaginary dangers to them and their rights by corporations in general.

JUDGE GEORGE W. WOODWARD[60]

As has already been indicated, one of the matters of primary concern at the time of the calling of the constitutional convention was the growth of corporate powers and abuses. This was not only reflected in

---

[54] The debt of counties, alone, in 1872 stood at approximately $50,000,000. Smull's *Legislative Handbook*, 1873, pp. 393-4. $44,000,000 of this was the debt of Philadelphia. See also editorial in *Pittsburgh Gazette*, November 9, 1872, entitled "Limitations of Indebtedness."

[55] Article IX, Section 8. Municipalities with an existing debt of 7% of the assessed valuation could be authorized by law to borrow an additional 3%; but any increase of 2% or more at any one time must have the approval of the voters. These provisions applied to counties, townships, boroughs and school districts as well as to cities.

[56] Article IX, Sec. 10.

[57] A section requiring all cities to have a mayor and council was approved on first reading, *Debates*, II, 395; also, a section defining the powers of the mayor, *ibid.*, p. 117. These provisions were, however, eliminated on second reading, *ibid.*, VI, 223, 224.

[58] *Debates*, III, 87, 88.

[59] *Debates*, VII, 751.

[60] *Debates*, III, 361.

the prohibition of special laws granting corporate charters, but also in a separate article in the constitution on private corporations.[61] Some of the provisions were carried over from the 1838 constitution, but most of the article was new. It was regarded by the convention members as "one of the most important divisions of the Constitution." It contained "many salutary regulations against abuse in corporate management and securities against monopoly and clique management."[62] It abolished all existing charters or grants of privileges under which bona fide organization had not already taken place and business commenced by the time of the effective date of the constitution.[63] This was a blow at the "floating charters" already described. Corporations were confined to the specific businesses for which they were established, and their charters made revocable when public interest should demand it. As a protection against watered stock and inside manipulations, corporations were forbidden to issue stocks and bonds "except for money, labor done, or money or property actually received." Any fictitious increase of stocks or indebtedness was declared void. All future issues of stocks and bonds must be in conformity with general law regulating their issuance.[64]

As a safeguard against "clique control" the cumulative voting plan was adopted for the election of corporation directors. This provision, Mr. Buckalew explained, would protect against any such exploitation by an inner circle of corporate management as had recently taken place in the "gigantic railroad swindles by the great railroad men of New York City." Had the cumulative voting system been required in New York, declared Mr. Buckalew, those stockholders who were defrauded by the "nefarious transactions" of the inner clique of the Erie Railroad would have had directors of their own choosing on the board. Such directors would have detected the schemes of the manipulators in time to call in the aid of the courts. Thus the interests of English stockholders and the estates of widows and orphans would have been protected, and the millions plundered would have been saved.[65]

A separate article on railroads and canals was included, and became the object of interesting maneuvers in the convention.[66] The fear of the growing power of the great railroad lines had been one of the pre-

---

[61] Article XVI.
[62] "A Statement and Exposition" in A. D. Harlan, *op. cit.*, pp. 171-2.
[63] Article XVI, Sec. 1.
[64] Article XVI, Sec. 7.
[65] *Debates*, VI, 37, 38.
[66] Article XVII.

disposing causes of the movement for constitutional revision. The railroad companies, as already noted, were well represented at the convention, but the anti-railroad delegates were a majority. This majority was determined to control the giant octopus, which was extending its tentacles into all phases of the economy, dominating mining, manufacturing, lumbering, and even real estate development. The fact that the legislature had full legal authority to set up the necessary safeguards did not deter the constitutional reformers. Apparently they did not trust even their reformed legislative body to respond to popular will on the subject! Doubtless they feared the railroad companies would continue as in the past to send their attorneys as members of the legislature.

The provisions reported by the Committee on Railroads and Canals were very largely borrowed from the recently adopted Illinois constitution and reflected the thinking of the "anti-railroad" delegates.[67] They put through their proposals with relative ease on first and second reading.[68] By the time the third reading was reached, opposition had stiffened. The pro-railroad delegates now became active, repeatedly proposing modifications and offering substitute sections. The defenders of the article, however, succeeded in forcing it through without any emasculating amendments.[69]

The beginning of the counterattack seemed innocent enough on the surface. Mr. Buckalew, who had voted with the majority, asked for unanimous consent to propose a substitute for section 7 of the article just adopted. His substitute section was substantially the same in content, but much more concise than the one approved. When unanimous consent was denied, he said that he felt compelled, alternatively, to move for reconsideration of the vote just taken on the entire article in order to make possible an improvement in the wording. This was granted by a vote of 45 to 36.[70] Only five of the delegates who had voted against the article now voted against the proposed reconsideration. All the major railroad men present voted to reconsider.[71] This

---

[67] The *Pittsburgh Commercial* scornfully stated that anything originating in Illinois was regarded by the convention as the perfect solution to problems. The Constitution of Illinois was, indeed, the "embodiment of all the constitutional wisdom of the age." See editorial, July 26, 1873, regarding article on railroads and canals.

[68] First reading occupied but a week, and little opposition developed on second reading.

[69] *Debates*, VIII, 38. The Article was adopted by a vote of 57 to 25.

[70] *Debates*, VIII, 39.

[71] Messrs. Knight, W. H. Smith, Cuyler, Lilly (of Lehigh Valley); Dallas (of the Reading). Mr. Buckalew was connected with the Reading. Messrs. Parsons, Lamberton and Fell were absent.

should have been a cue to the anti-railroad delegates. Immediately after the vote to reconsider, the convention adjourned for the day.

It was mid-October, and attendance at sessions remained slim. When the convention reconvened the following day, the pro-railroad delegates found themselves temporarily in a majority. They soon maneuvered to outflank their slothful opponents. After a series of attacks upon various sections had made it appear that the article really should be subjected to a careful rewriting, a motion was introduced providing for the appointment of a special committee to which the railroad article might be sent for such revision. After a brief skirmish during which the chairman of the original committee and one of his loyal supporters had expressed outrage at such a suggestion, the motion was adopted by a vote of 48 to 40.[72] After the vote had been announced, Thomas Howard of Allegheny County, a member of the original committee and vigorous critic of the railroads, stated bitterly, "My own judgment is that the power of the railroads has been evinced most wonderfully here today, and I am willing that what I say shall go upon the record."

The motion provided for a committee of seven appointed by the president of the convention, which should report on October 21. The committee was appointed the same day. Five of the members named to the committee were known to be favorable toward the railroads.[73]

Aroused by such tactics, the absentees who had assumed that their precious article was safely in the new constitution, hastened back to Philadelphia. At the October 21 session there was a larger attendance than at any time since the completion of second reading. The atmosphere was tense. As soon as the routine business had been disposed of, the chairman of the select committee reported its substitute draft. After a preliminary skirmish over the effect of accepting or rejecting the report, a motion was introduced proposing that the convention should resolve itself into the Committee of the Whole to substitute the original article for that reported by the select committee. Opponents of the select committee report denounced it in vigorous speeches, castigating the new proposal as one framed solely in the interest of the railroads. The tenseness was finally eased by a speech of Henry Carter, supporting the original article, which though not lacking in vigor was nevertheless lightened by humor. When the vote was finally taken the following

---

[72]*Debates*, VIII, 71. The Allegheny County delegation voted strongly against it.
[73]*Pittsburgh Gazette*, editorials, October 21 and October 23, 1873; *Debates*, VIII, 79.

day, the pro-railroad forces were defeated by a vote of 59 to 51.[74]

Debate on third reading on the original article was then renewed, but the reinstated original was finally approved on October 24 without significant revision.[75]

The new article declared all railroads and canals to be "public highways," and the companies operating them to be "common carriers." Such common carriers were authorized to operate their lines or canals between any points within the state, and to connect with or cross any other line. Such common carriers were forbidden to discriminate against the passengers or freight of other lines,[76] to discriminate between shippers or communities, or to charge more for in-state than out-of-state traffic.[77] Consolidations of parallel or competing lines were outlawed.[78] These provisions, especially those preventing discriminations of all kinds against competing lines, were staunchly opposed by the pro-railroad forces.[79]

Railroad and canal corporations were required to maintain public offices where information would be available and books kept open to inspection by stockholders and creditors. Such records must reveal the amount of paid-in capital stock, by whom it had been paid in, the names of all stockholders, and the names and addresses of officers.[80] The pro-railroad delegates denounced very bitterly this invasion of the privacy of corporations.[81]

In reply the chairman of the Committee on Railroads and Canals, which had reported the section, pointed out that railroad and canal corporations were not ordinary private corporations. They are "invested with public powers and functions which strictly private corporations do not possess." They exist for the purpose of performing certain public duties. They therefore are, he declared, responsible to the state and the people for the discharge of their duties.[82]

---

[74]*Debates*, VIII, 130-203.
[75]*Debates*, VIII, 304. The vote was 76-11.
[76]Art. XVI, Sec. 1. It was commonly charged, and enlarged upon in convention debate, that the Pennsylvania and other major lines charged higher rates for passengers and goods received from other lines; in many cases they had refused connections or declined to haul the freight cars of other lines.
[77]Art. XVI, Sec. 3, 7.
[78]Art. XVI, Sec. 4.
[79]*Debates*, III, 304-321.
[80]Art. XVI, Sec. 2.
[81]Mr. McAllister, *Debates*, III, 332; Mr. Mann, *ibid.*, III, 328, 9; Mr. Gowen, *ibid.*, III, 329; Mr. Cuyler, *ibid.*, III, 330; Mr. Wetherill, *ibid.*, III, 326, 327.
[82]Mr. Cochran, *Debates*, III, 322-4.

Other advocates of reform insisted that the provision was essential both to protect public interest and to protect stockholders against inside cliques. Railroads seeking capital, one delegate alleged, issued "all kinds of glowing prospectuses" indicating that their respective railroad lines were excellent fields for investment and that large dividends could be anticipated. When no dividends were paid, there was no way for investors to inquire into the financial condition of the railroad company. The public should have some means of determining the truth or falsity of glowing promises, and stockholders should have access to information regarding the management of the railroads in which they have invested.[83]

Another reform delegate insisted that the availability of the information required in this section was indispensable if mismanagement was to be eliminated. As matters stood, the controlling clique ran the corporations and kept the rest of the stockholders in complete ignorance. A director of one of the greatest railroad corporations had confided to him, he revealed, that the largest stockholders in the road could not get the slightest information regarding their stock, how much they themselves owned, or how much had been issued. Such conditions invited mismanagement.[84]

After prolonged discussion the provision was approved in a slightly revised form[85] and was accepted on subsequent readings.

The issuance of passes by railroad lines was outlawed.[86] Many of the railroad delegates opposed this provision, but Mr. Buckalew took issue with them, insisting that the free pass system had had iniquitous effects. Both judges and legislators had been influenced by this system.[87]

An attempt was made—it was in the original report of the committee—to make "all real and personal property of railroads" subject to taxation "for all purposes."[88] This drew the wrath of all railroad delegates and their sympathizers. In caustic terms they pointed to the preposterous results of having railroads taxed by every community through which their lines passed. They insisted that it would be far wiser to have the lines taxed but once, by the state, which relied primarily upon corporation taxes for its income. Mr. Knight of the Pennsylvania line insisted that railroads were already taxed more in Pennsylvania than in

---

[83] Mr. Campbell, *Debates*, III, 329-330.
[84] Mr. T. H. B. Patterson, *Debates*, III, 330-332.
[85] *Debates*, III, 337.
[86] Article XVI, Sec. 8.
[87] *Debates*, VIII, 291.
[88] *Debates*, III, 337. This was copied from the Ohio Constitution.

any other state in the Union.[89] Mr. Gowen of the Philadelphia & Reading also declared that the railroads were paying more than their share.[90]

Their opponents insisted that there was no reason why the railroads should be treated differently from others. They enjoyed all the benefits of local government, including police and fire protection for their property and access to the local courts to prosecute their civil claims. They should be made to pay for such services. Mr. Gowen had complained that the power to tax carried with it the power to lien the property of the lines, but the railroad critics scoffed at this. The railroads could easily avoid this hazard by simply paying the taxes due! They ridiculed, also, the claim that the railroads were disproportionately taxed. If their property was worth the amount represented by their capitalization, they were paying a mere pittance![91]

Mr. Buckalew suggested that it was wiser to leave the matter to the discretion of the General Assembly, permitting the legislature to determine which taxes should be levied at the state, and which at the local level. If corporations were subjected to local taxes, as proposed, the total amount of tax contributed by them probably would not be greater, but simply be redistributed.[92]

After considerable discussion of the matter, this policy was accepted by the delegates and the section was dropped.

Since 1873 was a panic year, it would seem probable that the debates and the constitutional provisions would have borne the scars of social unrest and economic uncertainty as had been true forty years earlier. The constitution however, had, been fairly well molded when Jay Cooke & Co. closed its doors in Philadelphia, New York, and Washington.[93] The full significance of this and succeeding events had not yet been grasped when the second reading draft was completed

---

[89]*Debates*, III, 388, 389.

[90]*Debates*, III, 337-341. Mr. Darlington also supported this position, *ibid.*, III 347-348; Mr. Lilly said that the railroads paid two-thirds of all state taxes, *ibid.*, III, 350, 351.

[91]Mr. Bartholomew, leader of the Schuylkill County Bar, delivered a dramatic address, pointing out the extensive powers of the railroad lines; he insisted that there was no reason why the railroads should not pay local taxes. *Debates*, III, 344, 345. Mr. Howard pointed out that the Pennsylvania Railroad with a capital stock of $100,000,000 paid a mere $184,000 to the state; but if it were assessed at the 20 mills assessed on property in Philadelphia, its local tax would amount to $2,000,000, *ibid.*, p. 368; Messrs. Biddle, J. P. Wetherill and Cochran expressed similar opinions, *ibid.*, 351-355.

[92]*Debates*, III, 365-366.

[93]*Philadelphia Public Ledger*, June 19, 1873.

and released to the press a week later. Indeed, newspaper editorials in the Pittsburgh papers pointed to the soundness of the economy in spite of the failure of major fiscal institutions. They pointed to the fact that the failures had not spread to productive industry.[94] The *Philadelphia Public Ledger* in its regular column, "The Money Market," did analyze the situation differently, but not until mid-September:[95]

The signs of the times are not in every respect propitious. While the country over is most prolific in the production of the great staples, there is visible all around us a pressure of debt, provoking financial distress at home as well as abroad. The debt is not in the main individual, but corporate. It is the debt of companies created in the construction of works of improvement years in advance of any necessity for their use.

A few resolutions dealing with labor problems were introduced early in the convention, but they were never debated. Had the convention been held a year later the problems springing out of the panic doubtless would have received considerable attention.

The convention met in an era of widespread agitation for temperance. The legislature of 1872, in response to popular demand, had put through a local option bill in spite of strong lobbying activities by the liquor interests. Petitions from all parts of the state flowed into the convention in a continuous stream, and several schemes were formally introduced. At one time the convention considered submitting a prohibition proposal to be voted on separately. This plan was accepted on first reading, but later was dropped.

It is interesting to note, also, that a proposal was introduced and debated on the floor which would have added to the Declaration of Rights an equal rights provision outlawing all discriminations on the basis of color. This provoked some lively argument and was, after discussion, rejected.

The Declaration of Rights for the most part was carried over verbatim from the 1838 constitution, but it was made the first article of the new constitution rather than the concluding article as in the past. A preamble was inserted, "recognizing the sovereignty of God, and humbly invoking His guidance" in the future destiny of the commonwealth. A few other changes were introduced. As has been noted elsewhere, the waiver of trial by jury in civil cases was authorized.[96] There

---

[94]The 1873-74 Report of the Commissioner of Labor Statistics stated that at least one-third of the work force of the state was unemployed and had been out of work for a year, but this was not anticipated in the summer of 1873.

[95]September 18, 1873.

[96]Article V, Sec. 27; the guarantee of jury trial "as heretofore," however, is con-

was vigorous agitation in the press for the strengthening of the guarantee of freedom of the press to protect newspaper editors from libel prosecutions for criticisms of the conduct of public officials.[97] The advocates of this reform did not secure as broad a guarantee as they wanted, but gained a partial victory in the modification of the section on libel.[98] The guarantee of free elections was strengthened by the additional provision that "no power civil or military" should at any time interfere with the free exercise of the vote.[99] The legislature was forbidden to make any irrevocable grant of special privileges or immunities.[100]

In the article on public education the public school program was broadened. The General Assembly was directed to provide a "thorough and efficient" system of schools for all children in the commonwealth above the age of six.[101] Thus was eliminated the distinction between pauper and nonpauper for which Thaddeus Stevens had fought in the 1837 convention.

The Assembly was further directed to appropriate at least one million dollars annually for the support of schools. This represented a substantial increase, since the last appropriation had been for approximately half that sum.

An attempt was made to provide for central control of textbook choice and to limit the frequency of change of textbooks, but fortunately these proposals fell by the wayside. There was also an unsuccessful attempt to make the superintendent of public instruction elective.

Women were made eligible for school offices. This was the only concession made to the efforts of the woman suffrage leaders.[102]

---

tinued in the Declaration of Rights, Sec. 6. For discussion in the convention see *Debates*, V, 694, ff.

[97]The *Pittsburgh Post*, for example, on November 25, 1872 carried an editorial calling upon the convention to remedy the "iniquitous, unjust and unpardonable libel law now in force in the state." The *Philadelphia Public Ledger*, May 22, 1873, urged the necessity of a more adequate constitutional guarantee.

[98]Article I, Sec. 7. The section added reads as follows: "No conviction shall be had in any prosecution for the publication of papers relating to the official conduct of officers or men in public capacity, or to any other matter proper for public investigation or information, where the fact that such publication was not maliciously or negligently made shall be established to the satisfaction of the jury; and in all indictments for libels, the jury shall have the right to determine the law and the facts, under the direction of the court, as in other cases." The *Philadelphia Public Ledger*, June 19, 1873, editorially complained of the inadequacy of this provision, though it acknowledged that the new provision was better than the old.

[99]Article I, Sec. 5.
[100]Article I, Sec. 17.
[101]Art. X, Sec. 1.
[102]Art. X, Sec. 3.

Amendments

The concluding article dealt with amendments. The convention continued the provision which had been adopted in the 1838 constitution requiring a majority vote in each house of the legislature for two successive sessions, followed by popular ratification. The restrictive provision, which denied the legislature authority to submit amendments more often than once every five years, was likewise continued.[103] A proposal that the people should vote every twenty years upon the question of the call of a constitutional convention was considered and rejected.[104] The constitution contains no provision regarding the calling of constitutional conventions.

[103] Article XVIII.
[104] *Debates*, V, 9.

CHAPTER 8: BATTLE FOR RATIFICATION OF THE REFORM CONSTITUTION

> *Until the hatred of the new Constitution arrayed the public servants against the sovereign will of the people, there was little activity among its friends; but now they are alert and resolute in every county of the state. We could fill a broad page every day with proceeds of meetings of men of both parties, extracts of newspapers of every sect and idea, and volunteer essays from distinguished pens. The unanimity of popular confidence in the new Constitution is as marked as the weakness of the opposition.*
>
> EDITOR, Philadelphia Press[1]

WHEN the new constitution was submitted for approval it received the active support of the liberal wing of the Republican party, which had endorsed Horace Greeley for the presidency in the 1872 election. The Democratic leadership was also wholeheartedly behind the movement for ratification. There were, however, some powerful forces aligned against the proposed new fundamental law. The leadership of the regular Republicans, generally called the Radical Republicans, with few exceptions was opposed to it. So likewise were the "row officers" in Philadelphia and their political henchmen, who were bitter over the constitutional elimination of the fee system of compensation.[2]

---

[1] Reprinted in the *Pittsburgh Gazette,* December 12, 1873.

[2] Senator A. K. McClure, who was an important political figure during the period, asserts that the leading row officers in Philadelphia received from $50,000 to $100,000 a year, "depending upon the measure of unscrupulousness in the exaction of illegal fees." A. K. McClure, *op. cit.*, 2, 352.

The manipulators of election returns in Philadelphia, allies of the "row officers," who were accustomed to counting in the right candidates, joined the opposition because the constitution abolished the registry law under which they had carried on their election frauds. Representatives of powerful railroad and corporate interests came out openly against it in the closing weeks of debate. Their spokesmen stumped the state against it. Many members of the bar, dissatisfied with the judiciary article, also joined the opposition ranks.[3]

The forces opposed to constitutional change did not wait until the constitution had been completed and submitted for public consideration to begin their campaign against it. Convention sessions had scarcely got under way before a syndicate of interests opposing reform bought two important newspapers, the *Pittsburgh Commercial* and the *Harrisburg Telegraph*.[4] The *Pittsburgh Commercial*, which had been giving full coverage of the convention proceedings, carried an editorial on January 27, 1873, which spoke regretfully of the departure from the staff of its esteemed editor, C. D. Brigham, who had worked faithfully through the years to build up the paper.[5] The new editor, Russell Errett, was a prominent Cameron politician.[6] Thenceforth, the daily reports of the proceedings disappeared, and the occasional reports printed were much abbreviated. Editorials under the new leadership characterized the delegates as "dreamers" and "vaguarists" and their work as the product of "tinkers." Proposals were frequently described as "silly" or "ridiculous." "No people with a gleam of intelligence," the *Commercial* editorialized at a time when only a few committees had reported their draft articles, "will approve of such an instrument." In a similar vein, late in February, Mr. Errett referred to the political "misanthrops and quacks, who seem to have got control of the Convention."

During the period preceding the referendum the *Commercial* intensified its bitter attacks upon the constitution and its framers, ridicul-

---

[3]*Ibid.*, pp. 352, 353. In Pittsburgh, however, 173 members of the Allegheny County bar, "including some of the best known lawyers," endorsed the constitution, *Pittsburg Post*, December 8, 1873. The same journal declared that a majority of the lawyers in the state were in favor of the constitution, that the railroad lawyers were the only ones opposing it (December 9, 1873).

[4]*Pittsburgh Gazette*, January 27, 1873; February 18, 1873.

[5]The *Pittsburgh Post* (Democratic), scornfully stated in its editorial column that Brigham was "consoled" for his loss by a $70,000 profit on the sale of the paper (January 16, 1873).

[6]The *Pittsburgh Post* alleged that the paper was now under the control of the "ring," that the purchasers were Errett, Mackey, Quay and Cameron. (January 28, 1873).

ing, criticizing, sometimes grossly misrepresenting provisions adopted, and belittling convention leaders.[7]

On December 6, as the ratification contest quickened, the leading editorial listed twenty-eight defects in the constitution. On the day of the election the *Commercial* called upon its readers to go to the polls and vote against the new document. The convention, Errett averred, had chosen an early date for the referendum deliberately before the people could carefully examine the constitution. Furthermore, the delegates had willfully deprived the people of the right to vote separately on the different provisions. "Teach the damagogues of the State that the people are sovereign," admonished the *Commercial* editor.

The *Harrisburg Telegraph*, as already mentioned, cast its vote editorially against the constitution. It charged that the adoption of the constitution was the first step in the removal of the capital from Harrisburg and, therefore, a threat to Harrisburg business interests. It charged that, pending such removal, the increased size of the legislative houses would necessitate costly reconstruction of the legislative chambers. It demonstrated "conclusively" that the new constitution would repeal the Act of 1866 which exempted real estate from state tax. As the day for the referendum approached, it editorially warned: "Let us pause and consider whether the success of the many valuable reforms for which

---

[7] The chief object of personal attack was Charles R. Buckalew, who was accused by the *Commercial* of being the chief author of the constitution. Attacks upon the convention itself carried such captions as, "How Not to Do It" (February 24), and "Worse and More of it" (February 25). Though the *Philadelphia Public Ledger*, the *Pittsburgh Gazette* and the *Pittsburgh Post* regarded the legislative articles as the crowning achievement of the convention, the *Commercial* mockingly declared: "What a fortunate thing it is that in spite of the villany that has crept into our legislature we have a body of exalted patriots in the convention who can put a stop to it and have thus been able to divine a remedy for it! Pennsylvania must have gone to certain destruction if she had not stumbled on 133 statesmen whom she had gathered into the Spruce Street Presbyterian Church." (February 1) Many provisions of the proposed constitution were misrepresented in editorials that appeared from time to time. The *Commercial* insisted, for example, that Article IX, which limits the types of real property which may be exempted from taxation, would repeal the state law which exempted real property from taxation by the state, and that under the new apportionment system it would be impossible for the Republicans ever again to elect a majority to the General Assembly! (November 12, 24) A week before the election the *Commercial* declared that the constitution would be opposed by: "Every lover of independence; every man who values secrecy of the ballot; every colored man; every owner of real estate; every lover of philanthropy; every lover of law and order." (December 8).

In all candor, the author must admit that, whatever the motives of the editor, his criticisms of the legislative character of the detailed provisions of many sections of the constitution were fully justified.

the instrument provides will be sufficient compensation for the abandonment of the great doctrine of popular government, and the danger to the life of the Republic which the adoption of the judicial article involves?"[8]

The *Beaver Radical* also joined the opposition. It was owned and edited by John Rutan, a Cameron politician. He had been for many years a leading Republican state senator.[9]

Most of the press, however, supported the constitution and urged all readers to go to the polls and cast a "yes" vote for the new fundamental law.[10] In Pittsburgh all papers, with the exception of the *Commercial*, were favorable. The *Gazette* and the *Post* were especially vigorous in their support. In addition to sympathetic coverage of the proceedings and publication of the text of the document,[11] they published almost daily during the latter part of the debate over ratification editorials explaining and defending provisions. The *Gazette* published a series of letters prepared by a prominent Allegheny County delegate expounding in detail the changes made[12] and explaining the reasons for their adoption by the convention. On the eve of the vote on ratification the *Gazette* published excerpts from favorable editorials which had appeared in newspapers throughout the state, showing the widespread support for the product of the convention.[13]

---

[8] Reprinted in the *Pittsburgh Gazette*, December 4, 1873.

[9] The *Pittsburgh Post* (November 15, 1873) included Rutan on its list of the "inner circle" of the state Republican "ring," under the leadership of Simon Cameron.

[10] The *Scranton Republican* stated that not more than ten newspapers in the entire state, most of them Republican, were opposed to the constitution. (Quoted in the *Pittsburgh Gazette*, December 12, 1873).

[11] The *Commercial*, on August 9, announced that it would not publish the text because it was too long. For favorable comment by the *Gazette* see especially the editorials appearing on November 17, 18 and 19, and December 16.

[12] The letters were written by David N. White. They appeared in the *Gazette* on November 24, 25, 27, December 2, 5, 1873. The *Gazette* also published a summary of the changes made by the constitution written by S. A. Purviance, also a local delegate (former state Attorney General); and reprinted the text of a letter written by Wayne MacVeagh for the citizens of Chester County (December 4, 1873).

[13] The list of papers from which the excerpts were taken is interesting from the point of view of the widely differing nature of many of the communities represented. All were Republican papers: *Altoona Tribune; Berks and Schuylkill Journal; Bradford Reporter; Butler Citizen; Coudersport Journal; Doylestown Intelligence; Greenville Advance; Lancaster Inquirer; Lawrence Journal; Lebanon Courier; Mauch Chunk Coal Gazette; McKean Miner; Mifflintown Sentinel; Monongahela Valley Messenger; Montour American; Montour Republican; Norristown Herald*

BATTLE FOR RATIFICATION OF THE REFORM CONSTITUTION

The *Gazette* joined the *Post* in taking to task the *Commercial*, the *Harrisburg Telegraph*, and the *Beaver Radical* for their opposition and in answering and ridiculing their criticisms of the constitution. On the day of the election the *Gazette* carried a first page editorial urging the people to get out and vote. The "Ring" in Philadelphia, the *Gazette* charged, was desperate and was reportedly bringing in repeaters from New York. The vote of all supporters of the constitution would be necessary to overcome the fraudulent vote.[14]

The *Post* was even more vigorous in its support. From the very beginning of the convention sessions the *Post* adopted a tone of sympathetic support and never once wavered in its loyalty. It was ever vigilant to answer critics and their criticisms. It looked upon the opposition as a conspiracy between the "Ring" and those interests which wished to control the legislature for their own purposes. It placed considerable emphasis upon the bipartisan character of the support for the constitution. It took pleasure in pointing out that all members of the Allegheny County delegation which had participated in the convention proceedings, Democrats and Republicans alike, had given their endorsement, and that the Democratic and Republican party chairmen in both Erie and Tioga counties had issued joint statements announcing their support. It took pride in the fact that many of the "very best citizens of Beaver County" had signed an address endorsing the constitution, and joined with them in the warning that defeat of the new document would set back reform for at least a quarter of a century.[15]

The *Post* gave extensive coverage to meetings and printed verbatim the speeches of distinguished political leaders who were backing the constitution. It devoted two and a half columns to a letter by ex-Governor Bigler "vindicating and explaining" the document. It also published in full the "Address to the People" of the Executive Committee of the convention and a similar address by the Reform Club of Philadelphia. As the day of the election approached the *Post* urged the people to speak by a 100,000 vote majority for the new constitution,

---

and *Free Press*; *Philadelphia Press*; *Pottsville Miners Journal*; *Reading Times and Dispatch*; *Scranton Republican*; *Sharpsville Advertiser*; *Stroudsburg Jeffersonian*; *Sunbury American*; *Tyrone Herald*; *Union City Times*; *Venango Citizen*; *Waynesburg Republican*; *Wellsburg Agitator*; *Westchester Village Record*; *Westchester American Republican*; *York True Democrat*. The excerpts were published in the *Gazette* on December 12, 1873.

[14] The *Gazette* estimated that at least 20,000 fraudulent votes would be cast in Philadelphia, and at least 80,000 more throughout the state.

[15] The *Pittsburgh Post*, November 17, December 2, 6, and 11, 1873.

and thus end the "Ring," the ballot box stuffers and the corruptors of the legislature.[16]

The *Pittsburgh Evening Chronicle*,[17] which boasted of the largest circulation in Western Pennsylvania, did not enter the fray until November, when the battle was joined in earnest between the opposing forces. During the long months of the convention sessions, the *Evening Chronicle* practically ignored the convention, its delegates, and the debates. Had the *Evening Chronicle* been the only source of information, its readers would scarcely have been aware that there was any convention at all! It ignored, also, the quarrel between the *Commercial* and the critics of that journal, the *Gazette* and the *Post*. It was not until mid-June that the *Evening Chronicle* took any editorial notice of the Philadelphia assembly. Then it reprinted an editorial from the *Philadelphia Public Record* supporting the change to biennial sessions and another from the *Philadelphia Inquirer* urging speed in the conclusion of the convention proceedings in time for the new document to be submitted to the people at the October election. In each instance the Pittsburgh journal indicated its approval of the ideas expressed.[18] It also published an editorial commending the changes in the libel provisions[19] and a brief statement of the limitations placed on special legislation.[20] It took no further notice of the convention or the constitution, however, until November. Then, in a leading editorial it declared its position unequivocally in favor of the constitution. The convention, it suggested, would never have been called had it not been for the abuses of the legislature, especially in regard to special legislation. The necessity was, however, a "great one." When a "deliberate body composed of the ablest and purest men of the state submit their scheme of reform," continued the *Evening Chronicle*, "it is as little as the mass of the voters can do to examine candidly the scheme and determine whether the merits do not greatly outweigh the flaws." The legislative sections, said the *Evening Chronicle*, embraced "a highly desirable plan of reform." If such reforms were faithfully carried out they would work a "beneficent revolution in the state."[21]

---

[16]The *Pittsburgh Post*, December 2, 1873.
[17]The spelling of Pittsburgh was not consistent at the time. Some spelled with the "h" on the end, others without. The acts of the legislature omitted the "h." The Pittsburgh papers, however, used the "h."
[18]The *Pittsburgh Evening Chronicle*, June 11 and 26, 1873.
[19]The *Pittsburgh Evening Chronicle*, June 19, 1873.
[20]The *Pittsburgh Evening Chronicle*, June 28, 1873.
[21]"The New Constitution," the *Pittsburgh Evening Chronicle*, November, 6, 1873.

This editorial was followed the next day by a two-column interview with a local convention delegate, who defended that body's handiwork.[22] Ex-Governor Bigler's letter was also published.[23] The *Evening Chronicle* also contributed toward the creation of the impression that there was a strong tide of public opinion rising in favor of the constitution. It reported that the Executive Committee of the convention, which was in close touch with political leaders of both parties throughout the state, had received information indicating public support from all parts of the commonwealth. It pointed to the widespread newspaper support as a further indication of strong popular favor.[24]

In Philadelphia, where most of the convention proceedings were held, the press gave fairly extensive coverage. There was an understandable tendency to emphasize the part played by Philadelphia delegates and to discuss more fully the issues of primary interest to Philadelphia. Since most of the smaller papers throughout the state could not send special reporters to attend the proceedings, they for the most part copied Philadelphia dispatches. Some supporters of the constitution were fearful that, as a consequence, the readers of the small town and rural press would gain a distorted picture, and be convinced that the great city interests were the chief concern of the convention.[25]

The *Philadelphia Evening Bulletin* was unfriendly toward the constitution, but the other major Philadelphia journals gave it their blessing, though generally in more restrained tones than the outspoken Pittsburgh champions of the cause. Among the leading supporters was the *Philadelphia Public Ledger*. It published regular reports of convention proceedings. These were bare accounts of sessions in the style

---

[22] Malcom Hay, delegate from Allegheny County.

[23] On November 10, in an editorial, Mr. Bigler's letter was summarized; on November 21, the full text was published.

[24] The *Evening Chronicle* reported that the leading papers in Luzerne, Schuylkill, Erie, Warren, Lycoming, Tioga, Huntingdon, Franklin and Adams counties and the majority of Republican papers in Lancaster county, were supporting the constitution. In Chester, all papers, and in Allegheny, of course, all but one were favorable. (November 18, 20, 1873.)

[25] The *Pittsburgh Gazette*, March 15, 1873, in a special dispatch from its reporter at Philadelphia, declared that the Philadelphia papers were "very imperfect" and gave "but a vague idea of the daily workings of the delegates." Since they specialized in reporting the speeches of Philadelphia delegates, they gave a distorted picture of the convention. "At best," said the *Gazette* reporter, "this [Philadelphia] is but an overgrown village, and the papers are typical of the people." Most of the Philadelphia delegates, he complained, were of like mind with the Philadelphia papers. They thought that the convention was for the purpose of reforming their city!

of an official journal, but were given first-page importance. From time to time the *Ledger* published editorials commending particular sections of the constitution. When the Committee on Legislation presented its report, the *Ledger* published an editorial on "The Convention's Great Work," which commended the proposed provisions as generally "wholesome" in character. The limitations on special legislation the editor found to be "supremely important provisions." If such provisions were adopted, he declared, "aggrieved and plundered communities, individuals and corporations would have some safety and rest."[26] When the provisions regarding representation in the state Senate were adopted, however, the *Ledger* editorially protested against the injustice done the city.[27] Nonetheless, when the fight was on in the courts the *Ledger* sided with the convention-appointed commission rather than the Philadelphia election officials.[28] When the day for the referendum arrived, the *Ledger* in a first page editorial urged its readers to go to the polls and cast a vote for the new constitution.

The tongues of orators, pens of delegates, and editorial columns of the press were not the only weapons wielded in the battle over ratification. Enemies of the constitution rushed to the courts to obtain injunctions, and the battle was temporarily adjourned from the forum of public opinion to the courtroom.

In Philadelphia court action was used to prevent the commission, which had been appointed by the convention to administer the election in that city, from superseding the regular election officials.[29] The opponents of the constitution felt certain that its ratification could be defeated if the administration of the election was left in the hands of the regular election officials. The convention leaders, fearing that the Philadelphia election manipulators might "count the constitution out," had in April sought enabling legislation authorizing the appointment of such a commission and the submission of the constitution at a special election. A bill for that purpose, drafted by Charles R. Buckalew, was introduced into the Senate by General White, who was serving

---

[26]The *Philadelphia Public Ledger*, March 3, 1873.

[27]March 6, 1873.

[28]The *North American, Star* and *Press*, and the *Germantown Chronicle* and *Germantown Telegraph* joined the *Ledger* in supporting the position of the commission.

[29]Under the Ordinance of Submission adopted by the convention, the commission was authorized to register the voters, since the existing registration lists would not be available; to appoint a judge of elections and two inspectors for each voting district; and to canvass the returns from the districts.

simultaneously as a delegate and a senator.[30] The bill was passed by the Senate without dissent.

When the bill reached the House, the Speaker, William Elliott, a Cameron henchman, left the Chair. Having taken the floor, he inveighed against the measure. In spite of his attempt to rally the Republican members to defeat the bill, it was passed by a two-thirds vote.[31] The next morning a Republican representative who had been absent when the vote was taken moved reconsideration. Having gained the information he presumably wanted, he did not press the issue to a conclusion.[32] The session ended a day later without a vote having been taken on his motion, but this was unnoticed by supporters of the bill in the confusion of the end of the session. Not until too late did they discover that they had been tricked. The attorney general ruled that, since the motion for reconsideration had not been disposed of by vote of the House, the measure had not been legally passed.[33]

---

[30]Senate Bill no. 1797.

[31]Elliott introduced an amendment providing for the submission of the constitution at the regular October election following completion of the work of the convention, and providing that the election should be held under the general laws of the commonwealth. This was defeated by a vote of 43 to 35, *Journal of the House*, 1873, pp. 1188-89. The bill was then approved on second reading. By vote of 54 to 26 the rules were suspended, and the bill was considered on third reading on the same day. The bill was then passed by voice vote. *Ibid.*, p. 1190.

[32]He moved postponement of consideration of his motion to reconsider.

[33]*Pittsburgh Gazette*, April 15 and 18, 1873; *Pittsburgh Post*, April 15, 1873. The hostile *Pittsburgh Commercial* presented the story in a different light, declaring that the bill was nothing less than a "Jesuitical trick" of Buckalew's. That gentlemen, they stated, had come to Harrisburg during the last week of the session, and had been very busy "hand-shaking and holding private conferences" with members of both Houses, especially with Democrats. Since he had talked only with his friends, the nature of his mission was kept very quiet. "No one assumed that he, of all others, had a little anaconda in his pocket that he wished to snake through" the legislature with railroad speed.

On one of the closing days of the session an adroitly worded bill was read in the Senate. Though apparently merely providing for the submission to the Governor of the proofs of adoption or rejection of the constitution, the bill really granted to the convention "full power and control over the whole question of the submission of the Constitution to a vote of the people." The senators, busy with their own bills, thought Buckalew's bill was harmless, and passed it without dissent. Mr. Buckalew then went to the transcribing room to see that the bill was sent over to the House immediately. When it reached the House, however, Speaker Elliott recognized the nature of the bill and sought to block it. So "insinuating and insidious had been Mr. Buckalew's personal labors there, that many of the Republican members were misled as to its real purpose" and voted for the bill. The next morning it was discovered that the bill was in Mr. Buckalew's handwriting, and that the real purpose was to set aside the election laws of the state. Notwithstanding the guile with which the bill was framed, it was clear that under its provisions the convention had the power to enact a new election law and to sit in judgment upon

The convention refused to be outdone by such chicanery. Adopting the position suggested by Mr. Buckalew,[34] it declared that as a constituent body of the people, it had full authority to determine the "manner of submission" of the constitution or amendments without the necessity of such enabling legislation. Besides, the Act of 1872 had already authorized the convention to determine the manner of submission. The Ordinance of Submission adopted by the delegates in November not only set the date for the special election, but also provided for the appointment of the commission.[35]

Early in December, opponents of the constitution instituted proceedings in the Supreme Court sitting nisi prius in Philadelphia.[36] The purpose of the suit was to obtain an injunction to prevent the special commission from performing its duties. On the eve of the court hearing the *New York World*, commenting on the "Pennsylvania Crisis," decried the legal action by critics of the convention. The commission appointed by the convention, the *World* argued, like the convention itself, exercised a power higher than that of the courts. If the court action succeeded and the injunction was issued, the *World* warned, the "Ring" would be free to manufacture its own returns.[37]

At the court hearing the interests of the commission were represented by Charles R. Buckalew, William H. Armstrong, and George Biddle, three of the prominent convention delegates. A fourth delegate, George Dallas, appeared on behalf of Philadelphia citizens wishing to intervene to defend the commission. The plaintiffs were represented by three distinguished members of the Philadelphia bar.[38]

---

the validity of election returns. Because of the dangerous nature of the bill, the motion to reconsider was made. Since the motion was not disposed of at the time of adjournment, the bill necessarily fell. (April 14, 1873)

[34]*Debates*, III, 245, 246.

[35]For text of the Ordinance see *Debates*, VIII, 724. This action drew the wrath of the *Pittsburgh Commercial*, which asked editorially where the convention got the power to enact law to regulate an election. The convention, the *Commercial* argued, had no authority to pass or amend laws; the convention had usurped the powers of the legislature. The editor called upon the people of Philadelphia to "refuse to submit to the insult heaped upon them by the convention." (November 5, 1873) The *Philadelphia Public Ledger*, however, endorsed the action, expressing relief that an honest vote would be assured.

[36]*Francis Wells v. Bain, et al.* and *Fitler, el al.*, and *Donnelly v. Fitler, et al.*, 75 *Pennsylvania State Reports* 39.

[37]The *New York World*, December 1, 1873, quoted with approval in the *Pittsburgh Post*, December 3, 1873. In Philadelphia most of the major journals sustained the commission and criticized the legal attack made upon it.

[38]Both Mr. Biddle and Mr. Dallas were members of the Philadelphia delegation at the convention. R. S. Ashurst, James E. Gowen, and B. H. Brewster represented

The plaintiffs charged that the convention had no authority to appoint the commission and that the Ordinance of Submission was itself defective, since under its provisions the constitution was submitted as a whole in defiance of a petition by one-third of the convention delegates for the separate submission of the judiciary article. Defense counsel argued that the convention, as a constituent body, had the authority to create the commission and confer the powers with which it had been invested. Counsel also denied that one-third of the members, in conformity with the rules of the convention, had petitioned for such separate submission.

In a unanimous opinion Chief Justice Agnew sustained the petition for the injunction against the commission, but brushed aside the objection to the submission of the constitution as a unit.[39]

The enemies of the constitution rejoiced over their victory. The *Pittsburgh Commercial* applauded the court and urged its readers to defeat the constitution, the "monster to which the Convention has given birth." The convention delegates had been so "intoxicated by their elevation to the task of Constitution-makers as to lose all regard and reverence for the law." They were, therefore, unfit to frame a constitution. The only appropriate answer to "such a gathering of law breakers and conspirators," declared the *Commercial*, was to reject their work.[40] Yet the *Philadelphia Public Ledger* denounced the decision as a serious blow to the rights of the people. "Stripped of its verbiage," declared the *Ledger*, "the foundation doctrine of the opinion could be stated thus: Except by revolution, the people of Pennsylvania have no power to alter or amend their form of state government except by permission of the Legislature." The *Ledger* further lamented that the "people have no right that the ring, the legislature and the railroad corporations, backed by the Supreme Court, are bound to respect."

Most of the press throughout the state was hostile to the Supreme Court decision and attacked Judge Agnew with such vigor that he felt

---

the plaintiffs.

[39] Justice Agnew argued that the convention was not a revolutionary body; that it had been called into being not by vote of the people under the Act of 1871, but by legislative action under the Act of 1872, which authorized the election of delegates. The convention was, therefore, bound by the provisions of the Act which had created it. The clear intent of the Act was that the election should be administered by known election officials already in existence. Hence, the convention had no authority to create the commission. The same Act did, however, give the convention the authority to submit the constitution or amendments "in such manner" as the convention should prescribe. This included the right to submit the document as a whole.

[40] December 8, 1873.

constrained to announce his intention of voting for the constitution.[41]

The second legal attack was made in Pittsburgh in the Common Pleas Court.[42] The action was in the form of a petition for an injunction to restrain the sheriff and the county commissioners from holding the ratification election in Allegheny County. The plaintiffs charged that the Act of 1872 calling the convention was unlawful since the constitution of 1838 contained no provision for such a call. They further charged that the limited vote plan for the choice of delegates violated Article II, Section 1 of the Pennsylvania constitution and Article IV of the national Constitution. The former provision required all elections to be free and equal, and the latter guaranteed a "republican form of government." They also alleged that the convention had been guilty of illegal acts in its revision and submission of the constitution: the convention had refused separate submission of the judiciary article; it had altered the Declaration of Rights; it had enacted an election law.

In an opinion answering the allegations seriatim, Judge Stowe, speaking for the court, denied the injunction. In commenting on the question of the right of the legislature with popular approval to call a convention, Judge Stowe asserted that "there is underlying our whole system of American government a principle of acknowledged right in the people to change their constitution, except where especially prohibited in a constitution itself, in all cases and at all times, whether there is a way provided in the constitution or not, by the interposition of the legislature, and the calling of a Convention as was done in the case in hand."[43] The friends of the constitution hailed this decision as

---

[41]A. K. McClure, *op. cit.*, 2, 252. The text of Agnew's letter was published in the *Pittsburgh Post*, December 8, 1873. Both the *Pittsburgh Post* and the *Pittsburgh Gazette* criticized Judge Agnew's opinion.

[42]*Robert Wood and Reese Owens, et al. vs. M. S. Quay*, in Common Pleas in Equity, December term, 1873, Judges Stowe and Collier sitting.

[43]*Wood's Appeal*, 75 *Pennsylvania State Reports*, at 65. In his opinion Judge Stowe pointed out that the absence of a specific provision for the calling of a convention had never been regarded as a bar to such a call. By 1865, twenty-five constitutional conventions had been held in states with no express constitutional provisions for a call. Thus the Acts of 1871 and 1872, by which the Pennsylvania legislature had submitted to the people the question of the calling of a convention and had subsequently provided for the election of delegates, were constitutional "unless something in the acts themselves" was "in conflict with some constitutional provision."

The opinion also denied that there was any provision in the Pennsylvania constitution which guaranteed that every elector should have the right to vote for as many persons as there were offices to be filled, or that the limited vote plan violated the national guarantee of a "republican" form of government. The charges of illegal action by the convention were swept aside by the judge as fallacious. Unless there is a limitation imposed upon the convention by the people when they

its enemies had the decision of the court at Philadelphia.[44]

With the battle of the courts over, the contest of words was resumed. In Philadelphia and Pittsburgh giant mass meetings were held where distinguished speakers urged support of the constitution, and smaller meetings for and against ratification were held throughout the state.[45] Simon Cameron belatedly came out for ratification. The *Philadelphia Press* scornfully announced, "General Cameron has at last discovered that there is a new Constitution to be voted for on the sixteenth of December, in the State of Pennsylvania, and that there is a strong likelihood of its being endorsed by the people. He does not hesitate to express his indignation at the course of the *Harrisburg Telegraph* in opposition to that instrument, and is particularly indignant at Mr. Russell Errett for taking the same side. They should have waited like wise men to see which way the people would go."[46]

The torrent of words, both written and spoken, came to an end on December 16, when the voters went to the polls and voted decisively for the constitution. They left no doubt of their desire for a change, casting a two-to-one affirmative vote. In Allegheny County the results were most spectacular. The constitution carried the county by a ten-to-one victory! In Erie and Butler counties in the west, Chester County in the east, Schuylkill and Berks counties in the hard coal region, and Huntingdon County in the south the vote ran well above the state average.[47]

Only ten counties rejected the constitution.[48] Snyder County cast a five-to-one vote against it, and Somerset and Greene counties

---

agree to call the convention, he declared, no such limitation can apply. It is "inherent in the nature of a constitutional assembly" that it has absolute power "untrammeled by mere legislative limitation" to propose to the people any plan they see fit. The objections to the provisions regarding the method of election, the opinion set aside as irrelevant, since they were inapplicable in Allegheny County.

This decision was upheld on appeal to the Supreme Court. The case, however, was not reached on appeal until after the constitution had been ratified. The opinion of the Court indicated that had the appellate tribunal been acting on the appeal before the people had approved, the Court would have sustained the objection to the revision of the Declaration of Rights. *Wood's Appeal, loc. cit.*

[44]In Pittsburgh the *Gazette,* the *Post* and the *Evening Chronicle* applauded the decision.

[45]*Pittsburgh Post,* December 8 and 12, 1873.

[46]Reprinted in the *Pittsburgh Gazette,* December 5, 1873.

[47]Erie produced an eight-to-one victory; Chester and Butler, a seven-to-one; Berks and Huntingdon a five-to-one; and Schuylkill a three-to-one victory.

[48]Adams, Blair, Dauphin, Greene, Indiana, Lebanon, Perry, Potter, Snyder, and Somerset counties.

cast a three-to-one "no" vote. Commenting on the pattern of voting on ratification, Senator McClure pointed out that the results were very difficult to interpret politically, since there were counties with heavy Republican majorities as well as Democratically controlled counties on both sides of the vote. The dominant mood for constitutional change, however, was unmistakable.[49]

---

[49] A. K. McClure, *op. cit.*, 2, 354. The constitution was adopted by a vote of 253,560 to 109,198, *Debates*, VIII, 733-34.

CHAPTER 9: AN EVALUATION OF THE REFORM CONSTITUTION

The Pennsylvania Constitution of 1873 guarantees that soldiers shall not be quartered in the homes of citizens in time of peace, that canals shall ever be held open as public highways, that citizens shall not be denied the right to bear arms; but it has no word to say on the vital issues of our time. Again and again as the people of the state have tried to cope with these issues, they have found themselves prevented from taking effective action by the dead hand of the past....   W. BROOKE GRAVES[1]

It is very difficult to essay an evaluation of the work of a different age, for inevitably one judges it in the cold light of later experience. An era trained to a different tempo finds it difficult to catch the beat of the rhythm that gave a past era its distinctive character and it is likely to be insensitive to those almost indefinable nuances that convey its mood.

Judged by twentieth-century needs, the constitution of Pennsylvania is inadequate and constricting. Much of the reasoning on which its provisions were based seems naive, some of it preposterous. No one today would argue that a legislative body could be made more honest—though some might insist, more representative—by being doubled in size of membership or that biennial sessions would eliminate lobbying by special interests. The ingenuity of man was much underrated by those who anticipated that legislative procedure could be controlled by iron-bound constitutional rules. No one today would expect to raise the level of political ethics by requiring a voter to sign his ballot. Subsequent experience has indicated that detailed limitations on legis-

---

[1] *American State Government*, fourth edition, D. C. Heath & Co., Boston, (1953), p. 65.

lative power, far from serving public interest, tend to weaken responsible solution of public problems. Certainly the delegates failed to deal imaginatively with the emerging role of the governor as a political leader.

If, however, one reads the press editorials of the time and attempts to probe the minds of the constitution-makers by reading the constitutional debates, one finds it difficult to pass so harsh a judgment as seems implied by such statements. Rather the reader comes away from such an experience with a feeling of appreciation of the pressing nature of the problems as viewed by the delegates and a keen awareness of the sincerity of the convention leaders in their attempt to eradicate the evils of their day. Though one must differ with the convention delegates in regard to the remedies prescribed, the problems they were designed to cure were nonetheless real. The state was firmly in the grasp of Simon Cameron and his organization, the "Ring," as the papers generally called it. Philadelphia and Pittsburgh, likewise, were under the control of local "rings," and charges of irregularities in governmental operations were frequent. The growing political influence of railroad and other corporate interests in this era of burgeoning economy; the sudden growth of urban communities with consequent city problems emerging in a period of newly developing public works and utilities; the persistent election scandals; the injustices resulting from backlogs on court calendars—these and many more were problems that required an immediate answer and were very real, indeed. So, likewise, was the blight of special legislation which like a black mold spread its mycelium beneath the political surface. The delegates were faced with problems new and old. For the new, there was no past experience to guide them. If they lacked creative imagination, they did not lack determination as they struck out on their new course. As faulty as the constitution is as a fundamental law, its defeat by the coalition of interests which opposed it for reasons of self-interest could hardly have served the public interest. With all its shortcomings, the new constitution had its merits. Senator McClure, who had lived and served the public under both the 1838 and the 1874 constitutions said of the reform document: "I have good reason to know that the general sweep of legislative venality was halted by the new Constitution."[2]

For the remainder of the century the constitution of 1874 served without amendment as the basic law of Pennsylvania.

---

[2] A. K. McClure, *op. cit.*, II, 421.

PART THREE

Twentieth Century Developments

CHAPTER *10*:

TWENTIETH CENTURY GROWTH

Day after day, year after year, we are awakened to the fact that science is making great and rapid strides to open up, perfect and develop every mystery of nature and its laws. Every new invention calls our attention to the vast and deep resources that must yet lie hidden in the womb of the future, and the possibility that generations yet unborn, will think how stupid, how ridiculous and barbarous were our applications and operations for locomotion and comfort or convenience of life. We judge this will be the case by a comparison of the past with the present, and a firm belief that science is in its infancy. Now we have before us advice of the making of a model which it is expected will astonish the world, as experiments are to be made with it, to show the practicality of propelling railway cars by electricity.
EDITOR, *Pittsburgh Gazette.*[1]

THOUGH one may assume the role of apologist for the constitution-makers who designed the cramped constitutional quarters in which the commonwealth still dwells, one may justly inquire whether a more commodious functional design would not better meet the needs of its family now grown to ten and a half million. The old home admittedly was designed according to the best architectural ideas of the age that produced it, an age which, as the *Gazette* declares, was astonished by the foreshadowing of the electric street railways. Now we Pennsylvanians, proud of our heritage, still climb its rickety stairways and peer through its narrow windows at the problems of an age that has witnessed such tremendous developments that it is beyond all astonishment!

---
[1]Editorial, June 8, 1872.

No better testimony to the need for constitutional revision can be found than in the frequency with which constitutional amendments have been proposed and the persistence of the movement for revision in spite of repeated popular rejection.

The convention of 1872-73 had rejected a proposal for the inclusion in the constitution of a mandated submission at twenty-year intervals of the question of the calling of a constitutional convention, but memories of the Philadelphia sessions had scarcely faded from the public mind before such a submission was made by the General Assembly in 1891.[2] The answer of the voters was an emphatic "no."[3] The amending process likewise lay dormant. No amendments were added or even proposed during the first quarter of a century of the new constitutional order. In 1901, however, the nineteenth-century spell was broken, and three amendments were adopted. This was but a modest beginning, ushering in a half century during which seventy amendments were submitted and fifty-one adopted. Since the turn of the half century mark ten more have been adopted and five rejected.[4] The amendments have varied considerably in significance, ranging from slight modifications in terms of office to authorizations of major borrowing by the state. One consisted of a complete metropolitan plan for Allegheny County. The most frequently modified articles have been Article VIII on Suffrage and Elections and Article IX on Taxation and Finance. None of the amendments has changed in a fundamental way the character of the constitution or of the system established by it.

The early amendments dealt primarily with suffrage and elections. In 1901 the provision for the signing and numbering of ballots, which the convention reformers had regarded as most significant, was eliminated, and secrecy of the ballot was restored.[5] At the same time the establishment of registration as a requirement for voting was authorized.[6] Laws regulating either registration or voting were required to be uniform for the same class of community, except that registration could be required in cities only.[7]

Eight years elapsed before any more amendments were submitted, then the voters were faced with ten proposals, nine of which were ac-

---

[2]Act No. 288, 1891 P. L. 345, signed by Governor Robert Pattison, June 19, 1891.
[3]The proposal was rejected by a three to one vote.
[4]For a complete listing of the amendments through November 6, 1956, see *Pennsylvania Manual*, 1957-8, Harrisburg (1958) pp. 75-7.
[5]Amendment No. 2, November 5, 1901, amending Sec. 4 of Article VIII.
[6]Amendment No. 1, November 5, 1901, amending Sec. 1 of Article VIII.
[7]Amendment No. 3, November 5, 1901, amending Sec. 7 of Article VIII.

cepted. By this series of amendments the municipal election was shifted from February to November, but the separation of state and local elections, established by the 1874 constitution, was retained. Municipal elections were set for the odd-numbered years and state or general elections for the even-numbered years. This change necessitated the adjustment of terms of some officials. The terms of county officers were changed from three to four years. The terms of the state auditor general and state treasurer were similarly changed to four years. Justices of the peace and Philadelphia magistrates were given a six-year term and their selection was set at the municipal election. All other judges were made elective at either general or municipal elections.[8]

In 1911, two amendments were submitted by the General Assembly. Both of them were local in application but required statewide approval. The first modified the municipal debt limitation of Article IX in so far as it related to the city of Philadelphia.[9] This was the first of a long series of amendments to the municipal debt provisions. At the same election the judiciary article was also amended. The number of common pleas courts in Philadelphia was increased from four to five, and the General Assembly was authorized to make future increases when necessary. The three courts in Allegheny County were consolidated to form one court.[10]

In 1913 the voters were again called upon to perform the constituent task. Five amendments were submitted at that time, but the voters rejected three of them. One of the approved amendments exempted self-liquidating projects from the constitutional debt limit for municipalities.[11]

The other amendment provided for an adjustment of the tenure of judges then in office whose term ended in the municipal election year. This was necessitated by the shift of the municipal election from February to November.[12]

Two important issues claimed the attention of the voters in 1915. All doubt as to the validity of the workmen's compensation law, enacted

---

[8]Amendments No. 1 to 6; 8 to 10, November 2, 1909, modifying Secs. 8 and 21 of Article IV; Secs. 11 and 12 of Article V; Sec. 3 of Article VIII; Sec. 1 of Article XII; and Sec. 2 of Article XIV.

[9]Amendment No. 1, November 7, 1911, amending Sec. 8 of Article IX.

[10]Amendment No. 2, November 7, 1911, amending Sec. 6 of Article V.

[11]Self-liquidating projects which for five years had met all costs were exempted from the debt limit by amendment No. 5, November 4, 1913, amending Sec. 15 of Article IX.

[12]Amendment No. 3, November 4, 1913, amending Sec. 3 of Article VIII.

by the legislature in 1915,[13] was removed by popular approval of the amendment on that subject.[14] The municipal indebtedness provisions were again amended.[15]

Three years later the voters approved the first of a long series of amendments by which specific borrowings beyond the $1,000,000 set by the constitution have been authorized. At that time they approved the borrowing of $50,000,000 for highway purposes.[16] Congress in 1916, as the imminence of war pointed to the need for more adequate transport, had enacted the Federal Highway Aid program. This federal nudging plus the growth of motor vehicular traffic prodded the legislature into proposing the amendment. It was popularly approved by more than a three-to-one margin. The voters at the same election ratified an amendment further modifying the municipal debt provision.[17]

Twenty-one amendments had been approved in eighteen years, and there were demands from various quarters for additional changes. Was the political climate not ripe for a constitutional revision? Many state leaders believed that it was.[18] Thirty years had elapsed since the voters had rejected the call of a convention. Those thirty years not only spanned the turn of the century and the first World War, but had witnessed a considerable growth in the population and the economy of the state. They had witnessed, also, an increase in state regulatory functions, a multiplication of state agencies, and a corresponding growth in the commonwealth budget. The need for a more adequate constitutional base seemed urgent. Governor Sproul, who had pledged himself as a candidate to support constitutional revision, appointed a Commission on Constitutional Revision to study the problem of constitutional reform and report its recommendations.[19] Its deliberations fill three plump volumes.[20] After a year's study the commission pre-

---

[13] Act of June 2, 1915, P. L. 736.
[14] Amendment No. 3, November 2, 1915, amending Sec. 21 of Article VIII.
[15] Amendment No. 2, November 2, 1915, amending Sec. 8 of Article IX. A third amendment was adopted which dealt with certain technical aspects of the registration of land titles. It was assigned no section or article number.
[16] Amendment No. 1, November 5, 1918, amending Sec. 4 of Article IX.
[17] Amendment No. 2, November 5, 1918, amending Sec. 8 of Article IX.
[18] See Dr. Francis Newton Thorpe, "A Constitution Outgrown," *The Pennsylvania Papers, The Pittsburgh Sun*, 1920.
[19] A commission of twenty-five members was authorized by Act No. 192, 1919 P. L. 388, signed by Governor Sproul on June 4, 1919.
[20] Pennsylvania Commission on Constitutional Revision, *Journal of Proceedings*, 3 vols., Harrisburg (1921). The chairman of the commission was William I. Schaffer, Attorney General of the state. The remainder of the roster included: A. Mitchell Palmer; Hampton L. Carson; James H. Reed; William B. Wilson; Edgar F. Smith;

sented a report to the General Assembly proposing 130 changes, touching almost every article and section of the constitution. Many of the changes were minor ones, but several were of great significance. Thus, the commission proposed an executive budget, state and local civil service, and a broadened educational program. The draft proposal strengthened the judiciary system at a number of points. It simplified the provisions for municipal debt limitation. It included a specific provision for the calling of constitutional conventions and made the amending process easier. Suffrage provisions were modified to grant women suffrage.

The commission did not, however, attempt to remedy the long detailed nature of the constitution. Its work was primarily a refining rather than a creative process. The constitution was thoroughly sifted to remove constitutional "clinkers," but apparently the spectacle of a legislative chamber in chains did not appal the commission members. Nor did the plight of the governor, whose effectiveness and responsibility were weakened by the limitation on succession, disturb them. Though the commission did propose specific modifications of some of the strictures on legislative power, it did not repudiate the principle of restriction. Thus, in its draft the commission authorized the legislative establishment of an exemption level for income and inheritance taxes, but did not remove the uniformity clause.[21] Increased borrowing for highways and for reforestration was authorized, but the general $1,000,000 debt limit was retained. Zoning regulations and excess condemnation were authorized. The constitutional strictures which presumably made such specific authorization necessary were not removed.

The draft proposal had the support of many men of distinction on the state political scene. Governor Sproul gave it his blessings. Senator George Wharton Pepper, who had served on the commission, endorsed it and urged public approval of a constitutional convention. Speaking at a civic gathering in Philadelphia, the senator declared:[22]

I believe this is the time ordained of God for the people of this commonwealth to revise our Constitution—to make our new resolutions for the

---

Edward J. Fox; Thomas D. Cuyler; George E. Alter; William Perrine; John Stackpole; George Wharton Pepper; R. L. Munce; James G. Gordon; Gifford Pinchot; John P. Connelly; Francis Newton Thorpe; Charles H. English; Chester J. Tyson; Mrs. Barclay H. Warburton; Mrs. John O. Miller. Mr. Palmer and Mr. Wilson resigned, and their places were taken by Vance C. McCormick and John A. Voll.

[21] A majority of the commission members were opposed to graduated state taxes, and therefore retained the uniformity clause.

[22] Address at the Bellevue-Stratford Hotel, March 1, 1921, published in leaflet form by the sponsoring committee.

future.... The time has arrived when a new day shall dawn in Pennsylvania, a new day educationally, socially, in respect to public welfare, in respect to municipal development, in respect to state activities, and in respect to responsible government.

Other members of the commission were active in advocating constitutional revision. The state Chamber of Commerce gave the revision movement its endorsement and expressed approval of the draft prepared by the commission.[23]

There were, however, misgivings on the part of some conservatives about constitutional revision at this time. They argued that the social unrest that always followed a major war was likely to produce a convention dominated by radicalism. They feared that such a convention might sweep aside the conservative provisions of the constitution. For this reason they felt that it would be dangerous to approve of the call.[24] There was dissatisfaction also among liberals, who felt that the commission had not gone far enough in removing conservative strictures. They therefore opposed the provision for the appointment by the governor of twenty-five delegates, a provision obviously intended to permit the governor to appoint the commission members as delegates. With neither conservative nor liberals satisfied, it is not surprising that the proposal was defeated by a 100,000 majority.[25]

Gifford Pinchot, liberal Republican, who came to the governorship in 1923, renewed the issue. He had served on the Commission on Revision and had supported the movement for the calling of the convention. Now as governor, he sought to spearhead the movement for change. A well-organized conservative opposition campaigned against the proposal, and the governor was rebuffed by a three-to-one vote against the call.[26]

Meanwhile constitutional growth did not stand still. In 1923 four constitutional amendments were adopted. The classification of municipalities on the basis of population was expressly authorized.[27] The $50,000,000 bond issue for highway purposes approved in 1918

---

[23]"Special Message to Members Regarding the Proposed Constitutional Convention" (signed by Alba B. Johnson, President); *Pennsylvania Progress*, September 8, 1921.

[24]Jacob Tanger, *The Pennsylvania Constitution*, Pennsylvania Book Service (1934), p. 11.

[25]Smull's *Legislative Handbook*, 1921-22, p. 763.

[26]Jacob Tanger, *loc. cit.*

[27]Amendment No. 3, November 6, 1923, amending Sec. 34 of Article III. In the midst of the revision battle the voters had approved a permissive "home rule" amendment (Amendment of November 7, 1922, amending Sec. 1 of Article XV).

was now increased to $100,000,000.[28] The other two amendments were of little constitutional significance.[29]

More important constitutionally than these amendments were two new developments put into effect in 1923 by legislative action under the militant leadership of Gifford Pinchot. Though enacted by law, not formal amendment, these measures so strengthened the position of the governor as to be of truly constitutional significance. The first of these was the executive budget system, which had been advocated by Governor Sproul's Commission on Revision. The 1923 Administrative Code not only vested the governor with responsibility for the preparation of the budget, but also under the allotment system established by the Code with the authority to supervise its execution. He was thus placed in a position of command in respect to the policies of all administrative agencies except the elective constitutional officers. Even the quasi-legislative Public Utility Commission, whose members he cannot remove, can be indirectly controlled through the governor's power to withhold funds.[30] The well-established practice of the General Assembly of passing the general appropriation bill at the very end of the session, with the consequence that it is impossible for the legislature to override the executive veto, has still further elevated the governor's position of control. This is all the more significant since, as already indicated, the governor has the power to veto single items, including the power to reduce items.[31]

The 1923 General Assembly also enacted an administrative reorganization program, championed by Governor Gifford Pinchot.[32] The new Administrative Code gathered together the 135 separate administrative agencies into fourteen departments and three commissions. The Code did not affect the constitutional officers elected by popular vote. Many of the legislatively created boards and commissions were

---

[28]Amendment No. 2, November 6, 1923, amending Sec. 4 of Article IX.

[29]The exemption of the property of veteran's organizations from the real property tax was authorized by Amendment No. 1, November 6, 1923, amending Sec. 1 of Article IX. Railroad companies, prohibited for half a century from granting passes, were now permitted to issue them to clergymen! Amendment No. 4, November 6, 1923, amending Sec. 8 of Article XVII.

[30]Art. VI, Sec. 601-608, Administrative Code, Act No. 274, 1923 P. L. 498.

[31]For an analysis of the effect of the default on the part of the legislature, springing out of its delay in passing budget bills, see M. Nelson McGeary, "The Governor's Veto in Pennsylvania," *The American Political Science Review*, XLI (1947): No. 5, pp. 941-46. For court decision construing the single item veto to include the power to reduce items, see *Commonwealth v. Barnett, 199 Pennsylvania State Reports 161.*

[32]Act No. 274, 1923 P. L. 498.

placed in the appropriate departments, but retained a measure of autonomy inconsistent with a program of complete consolidation. Nevertheless this reorganization strengthened the position of the governor as the head of the administrative branch.

After the court-enforced delay period of five years had elapsed[33] the amending process again was invoked. Fourteen amendments had accumulated. Of these the voters rejected ten. One of the four amendments which gained the voters' favor in the state-wide vote authorized a metropolitan plan for Allegheny County. This was an attempt to deal constructively with the problems of a metropolitan community splintered into a mosaic of third-class cities, boroughs, and townships, with Pittsburgh as its center.[34]

The other three amendments which survived the voter's hatchet related to the administration of elections. One authorized the use of voting machines; the other two modified certain details respecting the size of voting districts and the procedure in the creation of new districts.[35]

The five-year interval again produced a backlog of amendments by 1933. The voters were called upon to express their sovereign wish in regard to twelve amendments. The deepening shadows of the Great Depression made the voters more receptive to change, and they approved nine amendments. Three of the proposals approved by the electorate authorized borrowing beyond the limit established by the constitution. Thus approved was the borrowing of $50,000,000 for a soldiers' bonus for veterans of World War I, of $10,000,000 for acquisition by the state of toll bridges, and of $25,000,000 to meet anticipated deficiencies in revenue in the approaching biennium when the commonwealth would have to make increased welfare expenditures.[36]

---

[33]In *Armstrong, et al. v. King*, 281 *Pennsylvania State Reports* 207, the Supreme Court ruled that amendments could be submitted at five year intervals only.

[34]Amendment No. 14, November 6, 1928, adding Sec. 4 to Article XV. The plan was never put into effect; it was defeated in Allegheny County as a consequence of a "printer's error." The amendment provided that the charter would be put into effect if approved by a majority vote in Allegheny County, provided that it was also approved by a two-thirds vote in a majority of the communities. As originally drawn the amendment had provided for approval by a majority vote in two-thirds of the communities. Had the original provision been adopted the charter plan would have been put into effect. The change was allegedly a "printer's error."

[35]Amendment No. 3, amending Sec. 7, of Article VIII; amendment No. 6, amending Sec. 11 of Article VIII; amendment No. 12, adding Sec. 1b to Article IX.

[36]Amendments No. 4, 12 and 8, November 7, 1933, adding respectively Secs. 16 and 17 to Article IX.

The remaining amendments were a miscellaneous list, modifying sections in several articles. Blind pensions were authorized;[37] excess condemnation, recommended by the Sproul commission, was approved;[38] Philadelphia was empowered to levy special assessments against all property benefited by the building of subways and rapid transit railways, including non-abutting property.[39] A second metropolitan charter provision for Allegheny County was adopted as a substitute for the earlier provision. It was permissive rather than mandatory. The reform movement, rebuffed by the earlier defeat, did not regain momentum, and the new amendment failed to bear fruit.[40] The taxpaying qualification for voting was removed and Section 1 of Article VIII amended to conform to the Nineteenth Amendment to the national Constitution.[41] The other two amendments modified legislative provisions regarding trust investments[42] and discriminatory railroad rates.[43]

In the election of 1934 both Democrats and Republicans pledged themselves to put through a proposal for a constitutional convention. The deepening of the depression, pointing to the need for an increased budget at the very time when taxes were declining, indicated the urgency of a more adequate taxing authority and more flexible borrowing power. When the legislature met in 1935, control of the General Assembly was split between the two parties. The Democrats were in control of the House, but the Republicans had a majority in the Senate. Governor Earle in his biennial message urged the calling of a convention, declaring that "revision of the state Constitution is absolutely necessary."[44]

The Democratic House, insisting that the people had given a mandate for the calling of a convention, put through a bill providing for the

---

[37] Amendment No. 1, November 7, 1933, amending Sec. 18 of Article III.

[38] Amendment No. 10, November 7, 1933, amending Article XV by adding Sec. 5.

[39] Amendment No. 9, November 7, 1933, amending Article IX by adding Sec. 19.

[40] Amendment No. 11, November 7, 1933, amending Sec. 4 of Article XV.

[41] Amendment No. 5, November 7, 1933, amending Sec. 1 of Article VIII.

[42] Amendment No. 3, November 7, 1933, amending Sec. 22 of Article III, authorized the legislature to regulate by general law the investment of trust funds; the original provision forbade the investment of trust funds in stocks or bonds of private corporations.

[43] Amendment No. 7, November 7, 1933, amending Sec. 3 of Article XVII, removed the requirement rates for transit within the state should not be higher than rates for freight or persons transported in interstate transit.

[44] *House Journal*, 1935, p. 144.

convention without any provision for a popular referendum.[45] In the Senate Republicans blocked this proposal. They argued that the General Assembly had no power to call a convention without a popular referendum. The Senate forced through a modified proposal requiring a popular referendum and containing a restrictive provision regarding the constitutional limitation on borrowing power. The convention, if called, would be forbidden to increase the debt limit beyond $50,000,-000. Even with these safeguards some conservative Republicans voted against the proposal. Senator George L. Reed of Dauphin County, voicing their feelings, declared: "In view of the chaotic conditions now existing in the nation and in the state, no one can forecast into what dangers a Constitutional Convention may lead."[46] Democratic leaders reluctantly yielded, and the compromise proposal was agreed to.[47]

Governor Earle appointed an Advisory Committee on Constitutional Revision to prepare the soil for the convention.[48] The committee was a large body of seventy five members, including many political and civic leaders. Charles J. Margiotti, attorney general of the state, served as its chairman. William A. Schnader, former attorney general and Republican candidate for governor in 1934, was vice chairman of the committee and chairman of its committee on committees. The committee gave its report on September 12, just five days before the election.[49]

The Advisory Committee, like the Sproul commission before it, did not propose any major alteration in the character of the consti-

---

[45]House Bill 147. For the House vote, see *Legislative Journal*, 1935, p. 259.

[46]Pennsylvania General Assembly, *Legislative Journal*, 1935, p. 4119.

[47]Act No. 212, 1935, P. L. 604, signed by Governor Earle July 8, 1935.

[48]The committee met at Harrisburg on August 12, 1935 and appointed a Committee on Committees under the chairmanship of William A. Schnader. The committee set up eight sub-committees. The sub-committees and their chairmen were the following: Bill of Rights, E. M. Biddle; Legislature, Legislative Procedure and Future Constitutional Amendments, Judge William S. McLean, Jr.; Powers and Duties of the Legislature, Dr. Thomas A. Gates; The Executive, Dr. Elmer D. Graper; The Judiciary, Dr. William Draper Lewis; Taxation and Finance, Charles M. Morrison; Suffrage and Elections and Selection, Qualifications and Removal of Officers, Charles F. Uhl; Local Government, Wilmer M. Jacoby. Report of the Committee on Committees to The Governor's Committee on Constitutional Revision (unpublished mimeographed report). The full committee on September 12, 1935 discussed the recommendations of the sub-committees and unanimously approved a report to the Governor. The defeat of the proposed constitutional convention on September 17 resulted in the discontinuance of the work of the committee.

[49]*Report of the Advisory Committee on Constitutional Revision to Governor Earle*, Harrisburg, September 12, 1935 (unpublished).

tutional system. Thus, the committee recommended no change in the size or the frequency of the sessions of the General Assembly, nor did it propose any modification of the system of representation. It did, however, suggest several changes in respect to the powers and the procedure of that body. It proposed an express authorization of appropriations from public funds for relief grants, for the establishment of retirement allowances for state and public school employees, and for the reimbursement of denominational or sectarian hospitals for care of the indigent. It suggested the elimination of the requirement that bills be read at length on three separate days. It also provided in its draft for the exception of code laws from the constitutional requirement that bills should not contain more than one subject.[50]

The committee attacked with vigor the constitutional limitations on the fiscal powers of the legislature. Unlike the Sproul commission, the Earle committee favored graduated income, gift and inheritance taxes, and, hence, recommended that the uniformity clause should be modified accordingly. The limitations on state borrowing power the committee likewise singled out for modification, recommending changes in the constitutional limitations both as to maximum amount and the purposes for which borrowing may be undertaken. Though the committee favored an increase in the debt limit, it felt that the $50,000,000 suggested in the legislative act was too high. The broadened borrowing power, the committee proposed, should be tempered by the proviso that whenever the legislature authorizes any borrowing, it must enact the necessary taxes to service the debt.[51]

In dealing with the executive article the committee suggested that the number of elective officers should be decreased.[52] It recommended that provision should be made for closer cooperation between the executive and legislative branches. It felt that the budget system should be given the security of constitutional status.[53] The committee also proposed a compulsory civil service system.[54]

The local government provisions of the constitution were subjected to a variety of changes, broadening the powers of the General Assembly in regard to the classification of local units of government and

---

[50]Draft Article III. The Legislature.

[51]Draft Article VIII. Taxation and Finance.

[52]Only the governor, lieutenant governor and the auditor general should be elective. The committee also revived the proposal of the Sproul commission that provision should be made for determination of disability of the governor.

[53]Draft Article II. The Executive.

[54]Draft Article VI. Public Officers.

the reorganization of their structure.[55] The committee made express provision for metropolitan areas and urban counties.

The amending process, the committee advised, should be changed to remove the five-year interval provision except for amendments which had been proposed and rejected by the voters. An alternative plan for the proposal of amendments also was recommended. Under this plan amendments could be proposed by a single session of the legislature if passed by a two-thirds vote in each house. Amendments so proposed, however, would require a 60 per cent majority vote for ratification rather than the simple majority required for amendments passed by two successive sessions of the legislature.[56]

The popular referendum on the convention call was set for September 17, 1935, the municipal primary election. The issue of revision received widespread attention in academic circles. An entire issue of the *Annals* of the American Academy of Political and Social Science was devoted to "The State Constitution of the Future."[57] Most of the articles dealt specifically with the constitutional revision problems of Pennsylvania. Written by distinguished scholars and men of political experience, these articles portrayed vividly, for those who would read, the spectacle of a great commonwealth whose people were denied the right to choose the most effective means for solving the problems of the Great Depression, in modernizing the structure of local government, and in dealing with the multiplicity of problems which face urban government.[58]

The governor had hoped to avoid a partisan clash when he appointed Mr. Schnader as vice chairman. The Republican organization, however, came out emphatically not only against the committee draft, but against the convention call itself. Thus, Senator M. Harvey Taylor, speaking as chairman of the Republican State Central Committee, warned the voters of the dangers ahead if a convention were called.

---

[55]Some of the specific proposal follow: The power to classify should be broadened to include other bases for classification than population; the number of constitutional county officers should be reduced and the fee system of compensation abolished; proportional representation should be permitted in local government wherever the electors want it; the legislature should have broader powers in the authorization of excess condemnation and special assessments for public improvements; the legislature should have the power to provide metropolitan charters for metropolitan areas; cities and counties wherever coextensive should be consolidated. Draft Article VIII. Local Government.

[56]Draft Article IX. Future Amendments.

[57]*The Annals*, 181 (September, 1935).

[58]For a complete listing of these articles, see the bibliography.

He urged them not to be deceived by the $50,000,000 limitation on borrowing imposed by the act authorizing the referendum. The convention might disregard legislatively imposed limitations as had the 1872-73 convention. He warned them also against being misled by promises of mild reform. Such promises would not bind a convention. Joseph Grundy added the weight of his influence against the call. He felt that it was dangerous to undertake the revision of the fundamental law during abnormal times.[59]

Organized interest groups also entered the fray. The Pennsylvania Manufacturers Association, the State Chamber of Commerce, and the State Grange actively opposed the revision movement. A front organization, the Constitutional Defense Committee, sounded the alarm through an extensive campaign of newspaper advertisement. The Pennsylvania Bar Association straddled the issue. It released a report giving ten arguments for and six against revision. In defense of revision the report pointed out that without adequate fiscal powers the state would be unable to participate in the federal social security program. For this purpose the state should have broader borrowing power and should be authorized to levy graduated taxes. Other constitutional changes would also be necessary to make full participation possible. Improvements in local government structure, making possible a reduction in taxes, likewise could be effected only through constitutional change. The law-making procedure should be simplified. This reform would save the taxpayers hundreds of thousands of dollars. Furthermore, the 1874 constitution was not, in many respects, suited to twentieth-century conditions. On the negative side the report suggested that it was preferable that constitutions should be prepared during normal times. The device of short-term loans through the sale of tax anticipation notes rendered less irksome the constitutional limitation on borrowing. Indeed, the passage of the Tax Anticipation Act had made a convention unnecessary to meet existing expenditure needs. Until better economic conditions developed, it probably would be wiser to retain the strictures and thus compel a limitation on spending. Finally, the existing constitution had been clothed with legally defined meaning through court interpretation. A new constitution would create the necessity for a renewed process of interpretation with consequent uncertainties pending court action. Any necessary changes could be accomplished by amendment rather than revision. This would minimize the necessity for court interpretation. Though the Bar Association did not expressly

---

[59] *Pittsburgh Press*, September 13, 1935.

oppose revision the general tone of the report gave comfort to opponents of the proposed convention.[60]

Just as the Republican leaders were opposed to revision, so, in contrast, Democratic leaders supported it. Governor Earle in radio broadcasts and press releases gave his unqualified endorsement. "I have no desire to see revolutionary change in our State Constitution," he reassured the timid who shrank from the dangers of revision, "or to see radical changes in the nature of our government or public institutions." He pointed out, however, that "a different sense of social values" and of "social obligations" prevailed in 1874 than was acceptable in the current social order. Governor Earle declared that the state program demanded constitutional change. Such change was essential to make possible social security, efficient state and local government, and a sound school tax program. Senator Joseph Guffey pled with voters to support revision. "In the name of justice and common humanity, let us have a new constitution that will not stand in the path of liberal government," urged the Democratic senator. Such revision was necessary to remove constitutional doubt from social legislation and to make possible the tax program and long-term borrowing necessary to pay for an adequate program.[61]

There were many civic organizations and some economic interests that actively supported the proposal for revision. The League of Women Voters, the American Association of University Women, the Federation of Women's Clubs, the Urban League, the Pennsylvania Committee on Penal Affairs, and the Pennsylvania Security League were among those lending organization support. The Real Estate Board of Pennsylvania, which felt that the adoption of a state income tax offered the only possible relief for overtaxed owners of real property, gave its endorsement of the revision movement. The Pennsylvania Federation of Labor and the American Federation of Teachers also actively supported the movement.[62]

---

[60]*Pittsburgh Press*, September 13, 1935. *The Pennsylvania Black News*, August 30, 1935, published by the Pennsylvania Security League, reported that the State Chamber of Commerce had sent a letter to its members urging them to "use all reasonable and proper methods for the defeat" of the convention proposal.

[61]*Pittsburgh Press*, September 9, 1935.

[62]The *Pittsburgh Press*, September 15, 1935. The *Press* also reported support by several local organizations: the Legislative Council of Allegheny County, the Civic Club, the Real Estate Owners' and Taxpayers' League, the Women's International League for Peace and Freedom, the Council of Parent-Teachers Associations, the Pittsburgh Central Labor Union, and the Pittsburgh Teachers Associa-

As the time for the referendum approached the two state political organizations put pressure upon their respective precinct leaders to turn out the desired result. More than two million voters cast ballots on the issue on September 17, 1935. The forces of conservatism won out by a 56 per cent majority.[63]

The battle for revision was over, but the problems of the depression era still bore down with crushing weight upon the state government. Under the constitutional stricture on frequency of amendments as then interpreted the state could not borrow again until 1939. The state budget, which had stood at $335,000,000 for the last Pinchot biennium, now rose to $640,000,000. A broadening of the tax program was imperative, but under court interpretation of the uniformity clause an income tax with graduated rates was unconstitutional. The administration regarded a flat-rate income tax as inequitable. A general sales tax was rejected for the same reason. The state resorted to a variety of "emergency taxes." Faced by the financial crisis resulting from mounting costs in spite of the constitutional compulsion of a balanced budget,[64] state leaders discovered a means of evasion of the constitutional stricture on borrowing —the corporate authority. Thus the Turnpike Commission and the Pennsylvania State Authority were created and vested with the authority to borrow money on their own credit. The debt in each case was to be serviced out of charges for the use of the facilities provided by the corporate alter ego of the state. Accordingly, the Turnpike Commission was authorized to charge tolls for the use of the turnpike. The State Authority would likewise service its debt by the rentals charged for the use of the hospitals and other building facilities which it would construct and lease to the state.[65] This development set the pattern for later action, when the authority plan was adapted to the needs of local units of government. At the local level the corporate authority has made possible many municipal facilities previously impossible under constitutional debt limitations. It has also provided a device by which communities faced with a common problem can cut across local government lines by

---

tion. *The Pennsylvania Black News*, August 30, 1935, published by the Pennsylvania Security League with the endorsement of the Pennsylvania Federation of Labor and the American Federation of Teachers, gave vigorous endorsement of the proposal for a convention, and heaped abuse upon those opposing the call.

[63] The vote cast was 916,949 for and 1,184,160 against the convention call.

[64] In *Commonwealth ex rel, Schnader v. Liveright*, 308 *Pennsylvania State Reports* 35 (1932) the Pennsylvania Supreme Court ruled that appropriations may not legally exceed official estimates of expenditures by more than one million dollars.

[65] 1935 P. L. 452 and 1937 P. L. 774.

joining together in a single authority program. School authorities, water authorities, sewer authorities, and parking authorities are the most numerous, though there is a miscellaneous list of other types. By the end of 1957 the number of such authorities had risen to 1,110, with a debt of $979,000,000. During the first ten months of 1958 the number increased by about 8 per cent and the indebtedness rose above the billion dollar mark.[66] Meanwhile the Turnpike Commission debt had risen to more than $450,000,000, and the General State Authority debt to over $250,000,000.[67] Also at the state level the Pennsylvania Public School Building Authority, created in 1947, reported a bonded indebtedness of more than $100,000,000 in its 1957 *Annual Report*.[68]

Two years after the rejection of the convention, the voters returned to their work of patching up the old constitution. In 1937, they approved an amendment permitting pensions for blind persons, assistance for widowed mothers with dependent children, and pensions for the aged.[69]

In 1943 the voters provided for legislative control over the method of establishing election districts.[70] In 1945, they added four more amendments.[71] By one, they made certain that in future emergencies gasoline taxes could not be used for purposes other than highway programs. During the depression an "emergency" additional 1 cent tax had been levied for General Fund purposes. The voters now approved an amendment forever forbidding such a "misuse" of gasoline excises, dedicating gasoline taxes by constitutional fiat to the construction and maintenance of highways.[72]

By a second amendment the voters authorized the borrowing of

---

[66] Arthur R. Friedman, "Number of Authorities in State Still Rising," *The Pittsburgh Post-Gazette*, February 13, 1959, p. 24.

[67] Pennsylvania Turnpike Commission, *Annual Report*, 1957, p. 10; The General State Authority, *Annual Report*, 1958, p. 9.

[68] For a pro and con discussion of the public authority see Bureau of Municipal Research of Philadelphia, *The Authority in Pennsylvania, Pro and Con* (Philadelphia, 1949), and George G. Lindsay, "The Municipal Authority in Pennsylvania," *Dickinson Law Review*, v. 55 (1950-51): pp. 141-157.

[69] Amendment No. 1, November 2, 1937, amending Sec. 18 of Article III.

[70] Amendment No. 1, November 2, 1943, amending Sec. 11 of Article VIII.

[71] The Pennsylvania Supreme Court had reversed its decision in *Armstrong v. King*, 281 *Pennsylvania State Reports* 207 (1924), in which it had enunciated the "time-lock" interpretation of the five-year limitation on the frequency of submission of amendments. In *Commonwealth, ex rel. Margiotti v. Lawrence, et al*, 326 *Pennsylvania State Reports* 526 (1937) the court returned to the earlier interpretation of the provision, under which the restriction was assumed to prohibit the resubmission of an amendment already rejected.

[72] Amendment No. 1, November 6, 1945, adding Sec. 18 to Article IX.

$50,000,000 for broadly stated purposes.[73] Since borrowing under the earlier amendments had been in the form of serial bond issues, the debt had gradually declined so that at this time the net long-term indebtedness of the state stood at approximately $50,000,000, the lowest point in two decades. Under wartime conditions the corporate net income tax had yielded sufficient revenue to make possible the paying off of the debt of the General State Authority. The debt of the Turnpike Commission stood at approximately $51,000,000, giving the state a total indebtedness of little more than $100,000,000.

The borrowing authorized by the 1945 amendment marks the beginning of a reversal of the debt trend. Since 1945 state indebtedness has steadily increased, both through state borrowing in the form of general obligation bond issues and authority borrowing. In 1947, however, the voters placed a temporary check on the upsurge by rejecting an amendment authorizing additional borrowing for highway purposes.[74] By 1949 the public was in a more generous mood, as evidenced by approval of a $500,000,000 bond issue for a soldiers' bonus for veterans of World War II.[75] At the same election the voters ratified another amendment sponsored by veterans' organizations which broadened the absentee voting provisions for bedridden veterans.[76] A third amendment intended to encourage urban redevelopment through a tax-forgiveness provision was defeated.[77]

In 1951 approval was finally given to an amendment long desired by Philadelphia which completed the consolidation of the city of Philadelphia and Philadelphia County.[78] The following November the only amendment on the ballot was rejected. It provided for the borrowing

---

[73]Amendment No. 4, November 6, 1945, adding Sec. 21 to Article IX. Included in authorized purposes were: public buildings, highways, sanitary systems, reforestation, rehabilitation and hospitalization of veterans.

[74]Amendment No. 1, November 4, 1947, amending Sec. 4 of Article IX, rejected by a vote of almost 3 to 2.

[75]Amendment No. 1, November 8, 1949, adding Sec. 22 to Article IX. Of the amount authorized the commonwealth actually borrowed but $375,000,000.

[76]Amendment No. 3, November 8, 1949, amending Sec. 18 of Article VIII.

[77]This amendment, if it had been adopted, would have authorized the General Assembly by general law to exempt for a period not longer than twenty-five years property acquired by urban redevelopment authorities for redevelopment purposes. To this the voters, jealous of tax exemptions, said "no" by a substantial margin. The amendment rejected was Amendment No. 2, November 8, 1949 which would have amended Sec. 1 of Article IX.

[78]Amendment No. 1, November 6, 1951, adding Sec. 8 to Article XIV. Also approved at the same time was Amendment No. 2, amending Sec. 8 of Article IX, which modified the constitutional borrowing power of Philadelphia.

of up to $215,000,000 to pay off the indebtedness of the General State Authority and the State Highway and Bridge Authority. The object was to make possible the substitution of general obligation bonds for the authority bonds, since the former can be marketed at a lower interest rate.[79]

In 1953 voting by absentee ballot was authorized for physically incapacitated veterans who were not bedridden.[80] Three other amendments were rejected.[81] More significantly the voters rejected a renewed proposal for a constitutional convention. The ratio of disapproval was approximately the same as in 1935. General apathy, however, was indicated by the failure of more than 1,216,000 to vote on the issue. Opponents of revision had presented the proposal as a disguised scheme to add one more tax burden to the already heavy load on the taxpayers' shoulders.[82]

In 1955 constitutional doubt as to the validity of increases in retirement allowances for already retired commonwealth employees was removed by constitutional amendment. The postwar rise in living costs necessitated such an adjustment as a matter of justice.[83] In addition the voters removed the detailed requirements of Article XVI respecting the issuance of stocks and bonds by private corporations, leaving the regulation of this matter in the hands of the General Assembly.[84]

The next session of the General Assembly proposed three amendments, two submitted at the 1957 and one at the 1958 election. In 1957 the voters approved a soldiers' bonus for veterans of the Korean conflict,[85] and a general absentee ballot provision.[86] The legislature, however, has never passed the necessary legislation to make the absentee

---

[79] Amendment No. 3, November 4, 1952, proposing the addition of Sec. 22 to Article IX.

[80] Amendment No. 2, November 3, 1953, amending Sec. 18 of Article VIII.

[81] Amendments No. 1, 3 and 4, November 3, 1953, proposing, respectively, eligibility of county treasurers to succeed themselves in office, authorization of special tax provisions for privately owned forest preserves, and assignment in Allegheny County of County Court judges to sit in Oyer and Terminer and Quarter Sessions.

[82] The vote was 533,000 for and 683,000 against. There were approximately 5,000,000 registered voters! Bureau of Commissions and Elections, *Election Statistics*, 1954, p. 38.

[83] Amendment No. 1, November 8, 1955, amending Sec. 11 of Article III.

[84] Amendment No. 2, November 6, 1956, amending Sec. 7 of Article XVI.

[85] Amendment No. 2, November 5, 1957. This amendment, unlike earlier authorizations of borrowing, provided that the General Assembly must provide the necessary additional revenue to service the debt when it provides for the bond issue.

[86] Amendment No. 1, November 5, 1957, amending Article VIII by adding Sec. 19.

voting amendment effective. The movement for the adjustment of taxation to encourage forestry conservation, blocked in the past, was finally successful in 1958, when the tax uniformity clause was modified to permit the necessary departure from the existing constitutional stricture.[87]

In the recent election two amendments, one of them of considerable significance, were approved and one was rejected. Annual sessions of the General Assembly have been restored after eighty-five years, though on a limited basis. The sessions in the even-numbered years are limited to action on the budget. This makes possible an annual budget, which many critics of the biennial sessions have regarded as the most urgent reason for a change to annual sessions.[88] The sovereign voters also gave their approval to an amendment designed to avoid the disqualifying of otherwise eligible voters who have moved within sixty days of an election. Under the new amendment the voter may return to the election district where he formerly lived and was registered, and cast his ballot.[89] A third amendment increasing the borrowing power of school districts was rejected by the economy-minded voters. Actually this rejection, far from promoting economy, will result in higher costs in school construction under the authority system.[90]

Thus the constitutional tinkering has proceeded ploddingly as amendment has been added to amendment. Yet, when the tedious tale has been told and all has been weighed and examined, one will find that the constitution has not been fundamentally changed. It remains the same long, restrictive document. In fact, some of the amendments have rendered it longer and more specific. Eighty-five years have produced no adventurous experimentation, no imaginative approach to constitutional problems. Some of the changes adopted have been useful, but none has cured the basic weaknesses of the constitution.

---

[87] Amendment No. 3, November 4, 1958, amending Sec. 1 of Article IX.
[88] Amendment No. 1, November 3, 1959, amending Sec. 4 of Article II.
[89] Amendment No. 3, November 3, 1959, amending Sec. 1 of Article VIII.
[90] Amendment No. 2, November 3, 1959, proposing modification of Sec. 8 of Article IX, was overwhelmingly rejected by the voters.

CHAPTER 11:

AMENDMENT OR REVISION?

The fact that a majority of the constitutional committee thinks that 33 amendments are "critically needed," that 22 more are "very desirable," and that 68 more "would improve the language and form of the constitution," that very fact seems prima facie *evidence of how outmoded is Pennsylvania's 85-year old constitution . . .*

Maybe the time is still not ripe, psychologically, for the kind of constitutional overhaul that Pennsylvania increasingly requires. . . . But, the Committee on Constitutional Revision might have accomplished more long-term good for Pennsylvania if all its members had emphasized the need for a general revision of the state constitution and impressed upon the lawmakers and the people why such revision offers the most sensible solution to the problem.

EDITOR, Pittsburgh Post-Gazette.[1]

THE latest chapter in the story of attempts to revise the Pennsylvania constitution is only now unfolding. The Commission on Constitutional Revision, created by act of the 1957 General Assembly,[2] has completed its study and public hearings and has presented its report.[3] Its recommendations are now in the hands of the legislature. Only the future will reveal whether these proposals will bear fruit.

---

[1] March 11, 1959.
[2] Created by Act No. 400, 1957 P. L. 927.
[3] *Report of the Commission on Constitutional Revisions,* 1959, hereafter cited simply as *Report.* The Commission is to be commended on the format of its report. The recommended changes are presented comparatively with the existing text; each change is supported by a brief explanation of the reason for the suggested change. Minority recommendations are published with the report of the majority recommendations.

The commission, as provided by law, was composed of fifteen members, five appointed by the governor, five by the president pro tempore of the Senate, and five by the speaker of the House.[4] The Honorable Robert E. Woodside served as chairman of the commission.

The method of appointment foreshadowed a commission which would be predominantly conservative in outlook, one which would find unanimity difficult on issues over which conservatives and liberals differ. The *Report* the commission has presented is consequently a curious admixture of twentieth-century realism reflected in forward-looking, badly-needed reforms courageously endorsed, of a rigid conservatism unwilling to yield to twentieth-century needs, and of old-fashioned nineteenth-century liberal reformism. Thus, the *Report* recommends unlimited annual sessions and removal of unrealistic debt limitations, but leaves intact the constitutional barrier to a graduated state income tax. It admits the necessity for strengthening the leadership position of the governor by removing the bar to a second successive term, but declines to go all the way by permitting unlimited eligibility. It advocates elimination of legislative details inserted by nineteenth-century reformers and performs an admirable surgical removal of a host of such provisions. Nevertheless, it adds many new sections containing explicit details. In an intellectual retreat to nineteenth-century liberalism, it even includes a proposal for constitutional initiative. It proposes an impressive program of revision, but shrinks from the logic of a constitutional convention to perform the task.

The commission has refined its proposals by a classification of suggested amendments into three categories. Thirty-three of its reforms it declares to be "critically needed." Twenty-two more it has labeled as "very desirable." These, it suggests should be adopted by the regular

---

[4]Governor Leader appointed Miss Genevieve Blatt, Secretary of Internal Affairs; Richardson Dilworth, Mayor of the City of Philadelphia; Dr. Jefferson B. Fordham, Dean of the University of Pennsylvania Law School; Dr. M. Nelson McGeary, Head of the Department of Political Science, Pennsylvania State University; and Mrs. Robert L. McGeeham, Second Vice President of the Pennsylvania League of Women Voters. Senator Harvey Taylor, President Pro Tempore of the Senate, appointed Lieutenant General Milton G. Baker, Superintendent of Valley Forge Military Academy; Senator Robert D. Fleming; Mrs. Mitchell MacCartney, President of the Pennsylvania Council of Republican Women; Philip Price of Barnes, Dechert, Price, Myers and Rhoads Law Firm; and Robert Woodside, Judge of the Superior Court of Pennsylvania. Speaker Helm appointed Matthew A. Crawford, Vice President and General Counsel of Pittsburgh and Shawmut Railroad; George R. Lamade, publisher of *Grit*; Horace Stern, former Chief Justice of the Pennsylvania Supreme Court; O. Jacob Tallman, former State Senator; and Edwin W. Tompkins, member of the House of Representatives of Pennsylvania.

amending process! Even though, by gathering related amendments together in its draft resolutions, the commission has reduced the number of amendments to appear on the ballot to thirty-five, it has suggested a formidable task for the voters. If, in the popular referendum, the voters do not consistently follow the wisdom of the commission, the constitution may be left in a more advanced patchwork condition than at present. In addition the commission has recommended sixty-eight more amendments which "would improve the language and form of the constitution." These, it suggests, should be considered only in event that the constitution is completely revised. This difficult and extensive program of amendment and revision has been placed in the hands of the legislature. Though the commission has thus gone on record as favoring a considerable overhauling of the fundamental document, yet, surprisingly enough in view of the breadth of the program suggested, it has denied the imperative of a constitutional convention.

Summary of Recommendations

The recommendations of the 1959 report differ considerably from those presented by the Sproul and Earle commissions, and therefor warrant a careful scrutiny.

Included in the "critically needed" category were several proposals for the strengthening of the legislature. Unlimited annual sessions were recommended, with an accompanying provision that the General Assembly should be a "continuing body" during the two-year period for which the representatives were elected. This wholesome change would permit the General Assembly to perform more effectively its legislative tasks, especially in the fiscal area. Making the legislature a continuing body would prevent bills from dying on the calendar at the end of the first session of each biennium.[5] A second "critical" amendment would remove the restriction which prevents Philadelphia from having equitable representation in the Senate.[6] If given fair representation, Philadelphia would have ten senators, but under the present constitutional stricture it has but eight. Also included as a "class I" recommendation was a plan to compel the fulfillment of the constitutional mandate for reapportionment after each decennial census. The reapportionment of the House of Representatives in 1953 came after a lapse of thirty-two years. The Senate has remained immune from change since 1921![7]

---

[5] Amendment to Article II, Sec. 4, *Report*, p. 19.
[6] Amendment to Article II, Sec. 16, *Report*, p. 21.
[7] According to the plan suggested, if the legislature should fail to reapportion following the decennial census, the governor must call a special session for that purpose;

The power granted to the governor by the 1874 constitution to limit the subject matter to be acted upon at special sessions was part of the plan to limit the legislature to biennial sessions. With the return to annual sessions, the commission feels, this limitation upon special sessions is no longer desirable.[8]

The *Report* also contains numerous suggestions of "class II" proposals relating to the legislative branch. Thus, the commission suggested that bills codifying existing laws should be excepted from the proviso that no bill may contain more than one subject.[9] The constitutional requirement that all bills should be read at length on three separate days, the commission proposed, should be modified by the substitution of "considered" for "read at length."[10] It further proposed a more carefully defined section respecting incompatibility of offices for members of the General Assembly. Thus, it suggested that municipal, township, and borough officers should be barred from simultaneously holding seats in the legislature.[11]

In addition, the commission suggested the modification of several sections of Article III placing detailed limitations on the powers of the legislature.[12]

The commission found the executive article also in need of revision. Two "critical" amendments were proposed. The first would make the governor eligible for re-election for one successive term, though he would be barred from a third successive term. This change would, of course, strengthen the political position of the governor during his first

---

the legislature would be forbidden to adjourn *sine die* until it has enacted a reapportionment. Amendment to Article II, Sec. 18, *Report*, p. 22.

[8] Amendment to Article III, Sec. 25, *Report*, p. 23.

[9] Amendment to Article III, Sec. 3. This would protect code laws from the danger of being voided by the courts for breach of the constitutional restriction. Sec. 3 provides that no bill shall contain more than one subject. *Report*, p. 62.

[10] Amendment to Article III, Sec. 4, *Report*, pp. 62, 63. This modification conforms to actual practice; bills, as already explained, are never read at length.

[11] Amendment to Article II, Sec. 6, *Report*, pp. 61, 62.

[12] The commission proposed that Sec. 12 should be modified to require that all state purchases "so far as possible" be made under a system of competitive bidding, but the restriction which heretofore has made it impossible for the state to do its own printing should be removed. *Report*, pp. 64, 65. It also suggested that Sec. 16 be modified to permit cash refunds of overpayments of tax or license fees without the necessity of specific appropriations for such purposes. *Report*, p. 65. It also recommended that the present requirement for a two-thirds vote for appropriations for charitable and educational institutions not under the direct administration of the state should be changed to a majority vote. *Report*, pp. 66, 67. There was also a recommendation regarding Sec. 7 (25) which will be discussed in connection with changes in Article XVI.

term of office and would, as the commission suggests, give greater continuity to governmental programs. The governor, however, would be in the same position in dealing with his second term legislature as he currently is with his mid-term assembly. This seems to be an unnecessary restriction by the people upon themselves. Under the democratic process the people should be competent to choose or reject whom they prefer without such an arbitrary stricture. Experience at both state and national levels amply illustrates the weakening effect upon executive leadership of ineligibility for re-election.[13]

A number of "very desirable" changes in the executive article were also urged. Thus, the commission suggested that the secretary of internal affairs, the secretary of the commonwealth, and the superintendent of public instruction should be deprived of their constitutional status. The commission wisely rejected proposals that the attorney general should be made elective. They suggested those officers who were appointed by the governor should be confirmed by a majority of the Senate rather than by a two-thirds majority as the constitution now requires.[14] The commission proposed that the auditor general and the treasurer should be made eligible to succeed themselves in office.[15]

The judiciary system was subjected to considerable overhauling by the constitutional revisers. This is not surprising, since the commission membership included a former chief justice, a Superior Court judge, the dean of a law school, and several other members of the legal profession. Foremost among the "critical" changes suggested is a major modification of the method of choosing judges. The commission accepted the Pennsylvania Plan, long advocated by the Pennsylvania Bar Association. Under this plan, appellate judges and judges of courts of record in Philadelphia and Allegheny county would be chosen without partisan election contests. Other judicial districts would be given the option of adopting the plan for choice of their judges in courts of record. According to this plan, judges of the courts concerned, when their terms expired, would if they wished to be candidates for re-election "run against their records." The voters would simply vote "yes" or "no" on whether

---

[13] Amendment to Article IV, Sec. 3, *Report*, p. 24. Miss Blatt and Mr. Dilworth dissented in favor of indefinite eligibility for re-election. *Report*, p. 213.

[14] Amendment to Article IV, Sec. 8, *Report*, pp. 67-9. The change in the status of the three constitutional officers would entail the striking out of their names in Article IV, Sec. 1, where the constitutional officers are listed, and the repeal of Secs. 18, 19 and 20, where their duties are defined. *Report*, pp. 69-72. It would also make necessary the deletion of the name of the Secretary of Internal Affairs from Article VI, Sec. 4, *ibid*.

[15] Amendment to Article IV, Sec. 21, *Report*, p. 71.

they wished to retain particular judges. There would never be opposing candidates. In case of a vacancy caused by death, resignation, decision not to run again, or rejection by the voters, the vacancy would be filled in accordance with the new plan. The appropriate "judicial commission" would name three candidates, and the governor would name one of the three.[16] The governor's appointee would serve until the next general election, when the voters would have a chance to accept or reject the judge so named. Again, there would be no opposing candidate and no need for a partisan contest.[17]

The chief criticisms against this plan are directed against the restriction of the governor's choice to persons nominated by the judicial commission on which the legal profession would have a controlling voice. Appointment by the governor, after consultation with an advisory judicial commission, would be more compatible with the principle of popular control over policy-making.[18] Since the people would always have the power to reject the governor's appointee after the judge had had a short term on the bench, there would seem to be ample opportunity for the correction of errors in judgment or any political abuse on the part of a governor.

As an additional bulwark against political ties—which the advocates of the Pennsylvania Plan eschew for judges—judges are forbidden by an accompanying proposal to contribute to campaign funds, hold office in a political party or organization, or, while holding a judicial office, run for any other elective office in a primary or election.[19] Buckalew's highly prized reform, designed to prevent one-party control of the Supreme Court, the commission found to be incompatible with the scheme adopted. This the commission recommended should be repealed.[20]

The commission suggested important changes in the provisions respecting the minor judiciary. Though it failed to recommend the abolition of the justice of peace system and the alderman's court, it did recommend as urgent a reduction in the number of minor court judges and the

---

[16]If none of the three is acceptable to him, the commission must name three more.
[17]Amendment to Article V, Sec. 25. This program is written out in explicit detail in the draft provision (containing six subsections). *Report,* pp. 35-36. The proposed plan provides for a commission for the appellate courts and a separate commission for Philadelphia and Allegheny County.
[18]Unless one naively assumes that judges are not policy makers, but merely interpreters of the law, there is ample justification for the use of political processes in the choice of judges.
[19]Amendment to Article V, Sec. 25 (f), *Report,* p. 36.
[20]Repeal of Article V, Sec. 16, *Report,* p. 32.

substitution of a salaried basis of compensation for the present fee basis. In its *Report* the commission suggested that all judicial districts (except Philadelphia) should be divided into minor judiciary districts by the respective common pleas courts, and that the justices of the peace or aldermen should be chosen from these districts. Special provisions were made for Philadelphia. The present magistrate's court would be retained, but there would be an increase from 30,000 to 100,000 as the population base for a district. The common pleas court would have authority to prescribe rules of procedure for the minor judiciary courts.[21]

Since Pennsylvania had in 1934 removed the last substantive restrictions on suffrage, the commission had no major problems in this area of the fundamental law. The only change currently under serious consideration is a lowering of the age limit. This idea the commission rejected, preferring the retention of the historic "age of maturity" which applies in other areas of law as well. The only "critical" recommendation made in respect to the article on suffrage and elections was a proposal to permit qualified electors who have moved within sixty days of an election to return to the district of their former residence and vote.[22]

The commission subjected the article on taxation and finance to considerable revision. Significantly, however, the majority report made no proposal for modification of the tax uniformity provision. This failure is, certainly, one of the chief weaknesses in the report. The last four sessions of the legislature have been veritable battlegrounds over tax issues. The present session finds the tax program a thorny problem. The growing cost of state government demands a more adequate tax base. Modification of the uniformity clause, making possible a rational approach to budget problems, is imperative.[23]

The commission did, however, make recommendations for the removal of the crippling restrictions on indebtedness which have encour-

---

[21]Amendment to Article V, Sec. 11, *Report*, pp. 29-30. Sec. 13, incorporated into Sec. 11, would be repealed as a separate section.

[22]Amendment to Article VII, Sec. 1, *Report*, pp. 38-39. A similar proposal was approved by the voters on November 3, 1959.

[23]For majority recommendation, see *Report*, p. 139. A minority report signed by Miss Blatt, Mr. Dilworth and Mrs. McGeeham took issue with the majority on this point: "The failure of the majority of the Commission to recommend amendment of this section [Article IX, Sec. 1] is, in our opinion, a serious mistake. It is an omission which may vitiate much of the hard work done by the Commission in pointing out other but less fundamental modernizations of our basic law. . . . Amendment of this provision would, in our opinion, remove the shackles which have prevented the General Assembly from enacting modern and adequate tax legislation in the past. It would likewise leave the General Assembly free to modernize Pennsylvania's tax structure as future needs and conditions may require." *Report*, pp. 216, 217. Dr. McGeary qualifiedly endorsed the same ideas.

aged the growth of the authority system. The broadened power would be unlimited as to amount borrowed for capital improvement purposes, but approval of the people in a popular referendum would be necessary. Such borrowing would be secured by general obligation bonds. The commission also proposed that in such borrowing the commonwealth should use serial bonds. The million dollar limitation on borrowing for casual deficiencies in revenue would remain unchanged.[24]

Municipal debt provisions also were considerably modified in the report. This section of the constitution, complex in the beginning, has been rendered more detailed by a bewildering number of amendments added over the years. The commission suggested simply that no municipal debt should be incurred in excess of 2 per cent of the market value of the taxable property in any municipality without the approval of the voters. The same principle would apply to increases in the existing debt of a municipality. Under the commission proposal the General Assembly would have the power to set limits on local indebtedness by laws uniform for communities of the same class. Debt obligations serviced by the net operating revenues from designated projects the commission exempted from this provision.[25]

A slight modification of the sinking fund provision, which would make possible the sale of state bonds at a lower interest rate, was also proposed.[26]

The commission made some significant recommendations regarding the local government provisions in Articles XIV and XV. It suggested that, in place of the mandatory imposition of the "county row" officers, the General Assembly should have the power to regulate county government by general laws. The only restriction prescribed by the amended article is the requirement that the governing body shall be elective. The commission proposed that the specific details in the remaining sections of Article XIV should be repealed.[27] The adoption

---

[24] Amendment to Article IX, Sec. 8, *Report*, pp. 42, 43.

[25] Amendment to Article IX, Sec. 8; the new provision would make unnecessary Sec. 17 of the same article. *Report*, pp. 42, 43; 46, 47.

[26] The treasurer would be authorized to pay the necessary moneys into the sinking fund without the necessity of a specific legislative authorization. Amendment to Article IX, Sec. 11, *Report*, pp. 45, 46.

[27] Amendments to Article XIV, Secs. 1-7, *Report*, pp. 48-50. Draft Sec. 1 would authorize the General Assembly to provide for an optional plan. According to which the voters in a county could choose between two or more plans submitted by the legislature. The four year terms for county officers mandated by Sec. 2 would be repealed. *Report*, pp. 48-50.

of these proposals would make possible much needed constructive action in county government reform.

Similarly the commission recommended modification of the provisions of Article XV to permit the General Assembly to provide optional charters for cities and boroughs. It also proposed constitutional home rule for both cities and boroughs. Under the suggested home rule scheme the General Assembly would retain control over matters of "state concern" and municipalities have control over matters of "local self-government."[28]

The commission wisely recommended the repeal of Article XVII on railroads and canals, since its provisions are legislative in character.[29] It also proposed the repeal of the sections in Article XVI on private corporations which contained legislative details.[30]

The commission, as already noted, proposed sixty-eight amendments designed to improve the language and form of the constitution. Included among these is a revision of Article VII on oath of office. The commission draft restores the dignity of the oath as it appeared in earlier constitutions before the reformers of 1873 inserted their "iron-clad" test oath.[31]

Looking toward the future, the commission recommended several changes in respect to the amendment provisions of Article XVIII. It proposed the addition of a new section authorizing constitutional initiative.[32] In view of the recommended change to annual sessions of the legislature, the commission suggested that section 1 of the same article should be modified to permit ratification by two sessions of the same legislative body rather than to require favorable action by two successive legislative bodies.[33] It also advised the addition of a new section providing for the periodic appointment of a commission to review the constitution.[34]

The commission has performed a monumental service in its meticu-

---

[28] Amendment to Article XV by addition of Sec. 2, providing for the optional charter plan and Sec. 3 providing for the home rule plan. Section 3 as it appears in the draft is a detailed section covering many of the procedural aspects of the scheme. Unlike the present "home rule" provision, the new section would not simply authorize the legislature to provide for home rule. It would itself establish home rule. *Report*, pp. 50-55.

[29] *Report*, pp. 171-175.

[30] Sections 5-7, 9, 11-13.

[31] *Report*, p. 130.

[32] This was a Class II recommendation adding Sec. 2 to Article XVIII.

[33] *Report*, pp. 56, 57.

[34] This was a Class II recommendation adding Sec. 3 to Article XVIII.

lous examination of the constitution and proposals for revision. Though one may question the advisability of some of its recommendations and regret the omission of some badly needed reforms, its *Report* would serve as a useful groundwork for a constitutional convention. Considering the extent of the revision suggested by the commission and the "critical" nature of many of its recommendations, one would assume that the commission would wholeheartedly urge the calling of a convention at the earliest possible date. Nevertheless, the commission—and this is even more regrettable than any of the shortcomings in its specific revision recommendations—has declined to recommend a revision convention. Instead, it has proposed the achievement of its reform program by piecemeal amendment. This method presents almost insuperable difficulties. Even if the commission should accomplish the unbelievable feat of persuading the General Assembly to pass through two successive sessions the bulk of its proposals, it would have before it the far more difficult task of awakening public interest and persuading the voters to cast a vote on a bewildering long list of amendments. One may well ask whether the educational effort which would be essential to accomplish this would not serve equally well to create a well-informed public which would accept the necessity of a constitutional convention. Why should we hesitate to call a convention? Of what are we afraid? Of the democratic process? Of ourselves? If a convention is called, the delegates will be of our own choosing. The constitution which our delegates draft will have to be approved by us in a popular referendum before it can become the fundamental law of our commonwealth. Are we to assume that we, as voters, will conspire against ourselves to destroy our "sacred rights," as some vocal critics of revision have insisted? Pennsylvania has had four constitutional conventions during its statehood. None of the four destroyed the "sacred rights" recognized by the Charter of Privileges approved by William Penn in 1701. A present-day convention would be no less zealous in guarding "sacred rights."

The need for constitutional revision is urgent. The most practical as well as the most intelligent approach to modernization of our fundamental law is through the well-recognized system of proposal by a popularly chosen convention followed by ratification by the people.

BIBLIOGRAPHY

Books

Robert L. Brunhouse, *The Counter-Revolution in Pennsylvania, 1776-1790* (Pennsylvania Historical Commission, Department of Public Instruction, Harrisburg, 1942).

Charles R. Buckalew, *Buckalew on Proportional Representation* (J. Campbell & Sons, Philadelphia, 1872).

William M. Brigance, *Jeremiah Sullivan Black, A Defender of the Constitution and the Ten Commandments* (University of Pennsylvania Press, Philadelphia, 1934).

Edward Channing, *A History of the United States*, v. III (The Macmillan Company, New York, 1927).

Sherman Day, *Historical Collections of the State of Pennsylvania* (George W. Gorton, Philadelphia, 1843).

Wayland F. Dunaway, *A History of Pennsylvania*, 2nd. ed. (Prentice Hall, New York, 1948).

Francis A. Godcharles, *Pennsylvania, Political, Governmental, Military and Civil*, v. 1 (The American Historical Society, Philadelphia, 1933).

Howard M. Jenkins, *Pennsylvania, Colonial and Federal*, v. II (Pennsylvania Historical Publishing Association, Philadelphia, 1903).

Miles C. Kennedy and George H. Burgess, *Centennial History of the Pennsylvania Railroad Company* (Pennsylvania Railroad Company, Philadelphia, 1949).

Alexander K. McClure, *Old Time Notes of Pennsylvania*, 2 Vols. (J. C. Winston Company, Philadelphia, 1905).

J. Allan Nevins, *The American States During and After the Revolution* (The Macmillan Company, New York, 1924).

Howard W. Schotter, *The Growth and Development of the Pennsylvania Railroad Company* (Press of Allen, Lane and Scott, Philadelphia, 1927).

John P. Selsam, *The Pennsylvania Constitution of 1776: A Study in Revolutionary Democracy* (University of Pennsylvania Press, 1936).

Isaac Sharpless, *Two Centuries of Pennsylvania History* (J. B. Lippincott, Philadelphia, 1900).

Jacob Tanger, *The Pennsylvania Constitution* (Pennsylvania Book Service, Harrisburg, 1934).

George R. Taylor and Irene D. Neu, *The American Railroad Networks* (Harvard University Press, Cambridge, 1956).

William B. Wilson, *History of the Pennsylvania Railroad Company*, v. 1 (H. T. Coates & Company, Philadelphia, 1899).

Public Documents

Pennsylvania Bureau of Industrial Statistics, *Annual Report, 1872-73; Second Annual Report, 1873-74* (Harrisburg, 1873-1874).

The Proceedings Relative to Calling the Convention of 1776 and 1790, the Minutes of the Convention that Formed the Present Constitution of Pennsylvania, To-

gether with the Charter of William Penn, and a View of the Proceedings of the Convention of 1776 and the Council of Censors (J. S. Wiestling, Harrisburg, 1825).

Pennsylvania Constitutional Convention (1837), *Journal of the Convention of the State of Pennsylvania to Propose Amendments to the Constitution*, 2 Vols. (Harrisburg, 1837).

......, *Proceedings and Debates of the Convention of the Commonwealth of Pennsylvania to Propose Amendments to the Constitution*, 14 Vols. (Packer, Barrett & Parke, Harrisburg, 1837-39).

Pennsylvania Constitutional Convention (1872-73), *Debates of the Convention to Amend the Constitution of Pennsylvania, 1872-1873*, 9 Vols. (Benjamin Singerly, Harrisburg, 1873).

......, *Journal of the Convention to Amend the Constitution of Pennsylvania, 1872-1873*, 2 Vols. (Benjamin Singerly, Harrisburg, 1873).

......, A. D. Harlan, ed., *Pennsylvania Constitutional Convention, 1872 and 1873: Its Members and Officers and the Results of Their Labors* (Inquirer Book & Job Press, Philadelphia, 1873).

Pennsylvania Commission on Constitutional Amendment and Revision (1921), *Preliminary Draft of Constitution* (Harrisburg, 1920).

......, *Constitution as Adopted Nov. 9 and 10, 1920, Compared with Corresponding Sections of the Present Constitution* (Harrisburg, 1920).

......, *Journal of Proceedings*, 3 Vols. (Harrisburg, 1920-21).

......, *Report of the Commission to the General Assembly* (Harrisburg, 1921).

Advisory Committee on Constitutional Revision (1935), *Report* to Governor Earle (consolidated report of subcommittees, September 12, 1935, unpublished).

Pennsylvania Commission on Constitutional Revision (1958-59), *Report of the Commission on Constitutional Revision* (Harrisburg, 1959).

Pennsylvania General Assembly, *Legislative Journal*, 1935.

Pennsylvania General State Authority, *Annual Report* (Harrisburg, 1958).

Pennsylvania House of Representatives, *Journal*, 1873; 1935 (Harrisburg, 1873, 1935).

Pennsylvania Joint State Government Commission, *Organization and Administration of Pennsylvania State Government* (Harrisburg, 1941).

Pennsylvania Legislative Reference Bureau, *Constitutions of Pennsylvania, Constitution of the United States, Analytically Indexed* (Harrisburg, 1916).

Pennsylvania Turnpike Commission, *Annual Report*, 1957 (Harrisburg, 1957).

John A. Smull, *Rules and Decisions of the General Assembly of Pennsylvania*, 1872 (Harrisburg).

United States Census Bureau, *Ninth Census Report*, 3 Vols. (Washington, 1870).

Addresses, Articles in Periodicals, Non-Official Reports

Roy H. Akagi, "The Pennsylvania Constitution of 1838," *The Pennsylvania Magazine of History and Biography*, XLVIII (1924): 301-333.

Lorin Blodgett, "The Census of Industrial Employment, Wages and Social Condition in Philadelphia in 1870," address before the Philadelphia Social Science Association, April 23, 1872, printed in Pennsylvania Bureau of Industrial Statistics, *Annual Report*, 1872-1873, pp. 417-445.

Nelson Bortz, "The Molly Maguires," *The Pennsylvanian*, I (1944): 9-10.

Bureau of Municipal Research of Philadelphia, *The Authority in Pennsylvania, Pro and Con* (Philadelphia, 1949).

E. L. Burnham, "Pennsylvania Commission on Constitutional Amendment and Revision," *National Municipal Review*, X (1921): No. 3, 151-155.

Clarence N. Callender, "The Constitution of Pennsylvania: Should It Be Revised" *Pennsylvania Bar Association Quarterly*, XXIX (1958): 205-215.

Samuel Dickson, "The Development in Pennsylvania of Constitutional Restraints upon the Power and Procedure of the Legislature," *Pennsylvania Bar Association Report*. II (1896): 3-36.

P. L. Ford, "The Adoption of the Pennsylvania Constitution of 1776," *Political Science Quarterly*, X (1895): 426-459.

Arthur Friedman, "Number of Authorities in State Still Rising," *Pittsburgh Post-Gazette*, February 13, 1959.

James Geary, Governor, "Annual Message to the Legislature, January 4, 1871," *Pennsylvania Archives*, fourth series, VIII, 1127-1131.

Henry George, "Labor in Pennsylvania," *North American Review*, CXLIII (1886): 165-182; 268-277; 360-370; CXLIV (1887): 86-95.

Samuel B. Harding, "Party Struggles over the First Pennsylvania Constitution," *Annual Report* of the American Historical Association, 1894-95 (Washington, 1895): 371-402.

Gayle K. Lawrence, "General Appraisal of the Pennsylvania Constitution," Temple University *Economic and Business Bulletin*, IV (1951): 10-18.

William Draper Lewis, "Constitutional Revision in Pennsylvania," *American Political Science Review*, XV (1921): No. 4, 558-565.

C. H. Lincoln, "Representation in the Pennsylvania Assembly Prior to the Revolution," *Pennsylvania Magazine of History and Biography*, XXIII (1899): 23-34.

George G. Lindsay, "The Municipal Authority in Pennsylvania," *Dickinson Law Review*, LV (1950-51): 141-157.

M. Nelson McGeary, "The Governor's Veto in Pennsylvania," *American Political Science Review*, XLI (1947): No. 5, 941-46.

Pennsylvania Bar Association, "Report of the Committee on the Pennsylvania Constitution," *Pennsylvania Bar Association Report*, LVI (1950): 326-40.

Pennsylvania State Chamber of Commerce, "Special Message to Members Regarding the Proposed Constitutional Convention," (Harrisburg, 1920).

Pennsylvania State Association, *Reorganization of the State Government of Pennsylvania* (Philadelphia, 1922).

Chester H. Rhodes, Our Constitution and its Place in a Changing World," *Temple Law Quarterly*, XIX (1945-46): 27-37.

William A. Russ, Jr., "The Origin of the Ban on Special Legislation," *Pennsylvania History*, XI (1944): 260-275.

William A. Schnader, "Dead Wood in the Pennsylvania Constitution," *Temple Law Quarterly*, XXV (1952): No. 4, 399-409.

J. Paul Selsam, "The Political Revolution in Pennsylvania in 1776, *Pennsylvania History*, I (1934): 147-157.

Clarence Shenton, "Can the Legislature Alone Call a Constitutional Convention?", *Temple Law Quarterly*, X (1935): No. 1, 25-40.

Sheldon C. Tanner, "Constitutional Limitations on the Taxing Power of Pennsylvania," *University of Pittsburgh Law Review*, VII (1941): 98-113.

Francis Newton Thorpe, et al., *The Pennsylvania Papers* (The Pittsburgh Sun, 1920).

Irma A. Watts, "Why Pennsylvania Abandoned Unicameralism," *State Government*, IX (1936): 54-55.

Thomas R. White, "Amendment and Revision of State Constitutions," *University of Pennsylvania Law Review*, C (1952): 1132-52.

"Advocates of Constitutional Convention to Revise the State Constitution Declare Profound Changes in Business and Economic Conditions Call for Action," *Pennsylvania Progress*, February 8, 1921.

"No Rewriting of the 1874 Pennsylvania Constitution," *National Municipal Review*, XLII (1953): 563.

"Pennsylvania in its Industrial Aspects," *Republic*, II (1874): 261-68.

"The Pennsylvania Constitutional Convention of 1872-73," *The Penn Monthly*, IV (1873): 1-19.

"The State Constitution of the Future," *The Annals* of the American Academy of Political and Social Science, CLXXXI (September, 1935).

Note: Most of this issue was devoted to the problem of revision in Pennsylvania. A listing of the articles relative to revision in Pennsylvania follows:

Charles J. Margiotti, "Why We Must Revise the Pennsylvania Constitution," pp. 19-26; Herbert F. Goodrich, "Does the Bill of Rights Need Revision?", pp. 27-38; William A. Schnader, "The Constitution and the Legislature," pp. 39-49; Elmer D. Graper, "Public Employees and the Merit System," pp. 80-89; Robert E. Cushmen, "Our Antiquated Judicial System," pp. 90-96; Stuart H. Perry, "Shall We Appoint Our Judges?", pp. 97-108; Clarence W. Callender, "The Shackled Judiciary," pp. 109-114; M. Clyde Sheaffer, "A Commonwealth in Bondage," pp. 115-117; William J. Shultz, "Limitations on State and Local Borrowing Powers," pp. 118-124; Edward W. Carter, "The Pennsylvania Constitution and Finance," pp. 125-134; Franklin Spencer Edmonds, "Financial Aspects of Constitutional Revision," pp. 135-141; Murray Seasongood, "The Local Government Riddle," pp. 159-164; Harold F. Alderfer, "The Pennsylvania State Constitution and Local Government," pp. 165-169; Clarence G. Shenton, "The City in the State Constitution," pp. 170-179; Charles C. Rohlfing, "Amendment and Revision of State Constitutions," pp. 180-187.

Pennsylvania Black News (published by the Pennsylvania Security League), II, No. 1, August 30, 1935.

Files of the following newspapers (microfilm):

Pittsburgh Gazette, January 1, 1871—December 17, 1873.

Pittsburgh Commercial, November 1, 1872—December 17, 1873.

Pittsburgh Post, November 1, 1872—December 17, 1873.

Pittsburgh Evening Chronicle, November 1, 1872—December 17, 1873.

Philadelphia Public Ledger, November 1, 1872—December 17, 1873.

INDEX

A

Administrative Code, 133
Advisory Commission on Constitutional Revision (1935), 136-38
Agnew, Daniel: delegate to convention of 1837, 23; opinion in *Wells v. Bain,* 118, 119; support for constitution of 1874, 119, 120
Amending process, 31, 108, 138, 155; court interpretation of, 134, 142
American Stores Co. v. Boardman, 336 Pa. 36 (1939), 66
Annual sessions, 14, 20, 68, 145, 149
Anti-Constitutionalists, 17-19
Anti-Masonic party, 22, 31
Anti-Proprietary party, 10
Apportionment (legislative), 14, 20, 70-74, 149
Armstrong, William H., delegate to the convention of 1872-73: committee on judiciary report, 79-80; counsel for Philadelphia election commission, 118; *remarks on* selection of judges, 81, 82, separate submission of Judiciary Article, 86
Armstrong et al v. King, 281 Pa. 207 (1924), 134, 142
Attorney General, 75, 76, 151
Auditor General, 75, 129, 151

B

Banks and banking, 26, 29, 30, 41, 43
Baltimore and Ohio Railroad, 44, 45
Beaver Radical: opposition to constitution of 1874, 112
Biddle, George, delegate to convention of 1872-73, 68, 73, 90, 105, 118
Biddle, James, delegate to convention of 1837, 23
Bigler, William, governor of Pennsylvania (1852-55): delegate to convention of 1872-73, 60, 62, 113, 115; biographical note, 60
Black, Jeremiah, chief justice of Pennsylvania Supreme Court (1851-55): delegate to convention of 1872-73, 60, 63, 69, 70; biographical note, 60
Blind pensions, 135, 142
Blodgett, Lorin, 50, 51
Board of Pardons, 75, 76
Borrowing power (state): constitutional restriction of, 32, 130, 132, 134, 136, 142, 143, 144; revision recommendations regarding, 131, 137, 153, 154
Broomall, John, delegate to convention of 1872-73: opposition to biennial sessions, 67; *remarks on* circuit court, 80, 81, woman suffrage, 94-96
Bryan, George, delegate to convention of 1776, 13, 14
Buckalew, Charles R., delegate to convention of 1872-73: biographical note, 60, 61; candidate for governor, 57; chairman of committee on public and municipal debts, 63; counsel for Philadelphia election commission, 118; *position respecting* appropriations to charitable institutions, 66, ballot secrecy and reforms, 89, 91, biennial sessions, 68, cumulative voting, 87, eligibility of governor to succeed himself, 76, limited vote plan, 78, 97, 100, railroad passes, prohibition of, 104, railroad taxation, 105, reconsideration of railroad article, 101; sponsor of bill for convention supervision of ratification election, 117, 118
Budget (state): adoption of, 133; growth of, 141; recommendation of commissions on constitutional revision respecting, 131, 137

C

Cameron, Simon, 54, 59, 60, 110, 112, 117, 121, 124
Cannon, James, delegate to the convention of 1776, 13, 14
Chauncey, Charles, delegate to convention of 1837, 22, 25, 26, 28
Chesterman Commission, 6
Circuit Court: created by constitution of 1790, 20; destroyed by constitution of

161

1838, 30; revival defeated in convention of 1872-73, 79-81

Civil service, 131, 137

Civil War: influence on Pennsylvania economy, 38, 39, 44, 50, 52, 54

Clymer, George, delegate to convention of 1776, 13

Coal industry: employment conditions in, 51, 52; growth of in Pennsylvania (1860-70), 40

Commission on Constitutional Revision (1958-59); creation and appointment, 147, 148; recommendations, 149-55

Commissioner of Labor Statistics (Pennsylvania), 48, 49

Committee of correspondence, 12

Common Pleas Court, 15, 20, 30, 78, 85, 129

Commonwealth, appellant v. Barnett, 199 Pa. 161 (1901), 133

Commonwealth ex rel. Margiotti v. Lawrence, 326 Pa. 526 (1937), 142

Commonwealth ex rel. Schnader v. Liveright, 308 Pa. 35 (1932), 141

Constitution of 1776: adoption of, 16; *provisions respecting* Council of Censors, 15, Declaration of Rights, 14, executive council, 14, 15, judiciary, 15, legislature, 14, suffrage, 14; revision, movement for, 17-19

Constitution of 1790: adoption of, 20; *provisions respecting* Declaration of Rights, 20, governor's office, 19, judiciary, 20, legislature, 19, 20, suffrage, 20; revision, movement for, 21, 22

Constitution of 1838: amendments to, 31, 32; *provisions respecting* amending process, 31, Declaration of Rights, 20, education, 29, executive, 29, 30, judiciary, 30, legislature, 30, suffrage, 30, 31; ratification of, 31

Constitution of 1874: amendments to, 128-30, 132-35, 142-45; *provisions respecting* amending process, 108, corporations, railroads and canals, 100-4, Declaration of Rights, 106, 107, education, 107, executive, 75, 76, judiciary, 77, 78, legislature, 65-68, 70, 74, local government, 96-99, suffrage and elections, 92, 93; ratification of, 121, 122

Constitutional convention of 1776: convention delegates and leaders, 13; political movement for, 9-13; popular referendum on, 13; work of, 14-16

Constitutional convention of 1789-90: call of, 19; delegates and leaders, 19; work of, 19, 20

Constitutional convention of 1837: call of, 22; delegates and leaders, 22, 23; *debates on* amending process, 31, corporations and banking, 26-29, education, 29, executive, 24, judiciary, 24, 25; political movement for, 21, 22; provisions adopted, 29-31

Constitutional convention of 1872-73: apportionment and election, 57; call, 56; *debates on* amending process, 108, corporations, 99, 100, Declaration of Rights, 106, 107, education, 107, executive, 74-77, judiciary, 77-86, legislature, 65-74, local government, 96-99, railroads and canals, 100-5; suffrage and elections, 87-96; temperance, 106; Ordinance of Submission, 64; organization and rules, 57, 58, 62, 63; movement for, 55, 56; sessions, 63, 64

Constitutional Defense Committee, 139

Constitutional revision: *popular referendum on* (1891), 128, (1921), 132, (1923), 132, (1935), 141, (1953), 144; revision movement, 128, 130-32, 135-41, 144, 147-49

Constitutionalists, 17, 18, 19

Corporations, 26-29, 30, 41-43, 100, 144; recommendations of 1959 commission on revision regarding, 155

Council of Censors: constitutional provision for (1776), 15; defeat of convention call, 18; majority and minority reports, 18; sessions, 18, 19

Counties: creation of regulated, 32, 96, 97

County officers, 24, 29, 97, 129; recommendations of commissions on revision regarding, 138, 154, 155

Craig, David, delegate to convention of 1872-73, 73, 77

Curtin, Andrew G., governor of Pennsylvania (1861-67), delegate to convention of 1872-73: biographical note, 60; chairman of committee on executive, 63; influence in convention, 75, 76; *position respecting* executive powers, 74, viva voce voting, 89

Cuyler, Theodore, delegate to convention of 1872-73, 60, 62, 73, 101

D

Darlington, William, delegate to conventions of 1837 and 1872-73, 61, 67, 68, 70, 95, 105

Dickey, John, delegate to convention of 1837, 23, 25

Dickinson, John: resolution condemning constitution of 1776, 16

E

Earle, George, governor of Pennsylvania (1935-39): appointment of Advisory Committee on Constitutional Revision, 136; biennial message, 135; radio address supporting convention call, 140

Education, 29, 53, 107, 131

Election irregularities, 87-92

Elections provisions: absentee ballots, 32, 143, 144; date of elections, 92, 129; registration, 128; signing and numbering of ballots, 92, 128; voting districts, 134; voting machines, 134

Elliott, William, 117

Errett, Russell, 110, 111, 121

Excess condemnation, 131, 135

Executive branch: constitutional provisions, 14, 15, 19, 29, 30, 75, 76; debates in Council of Censors, 18, convention of 1837, 23, 24, convention of 1872-73, 74-76; Executive Council created, 14, 15; governor's office revived, 19; power of appointment reduced, 29, 30; recommendations of commissions on revision, 131, 137, 150, 151; succession limited, 76; veto power strengthened, 75

F

Floating charters, 42, 100

Franklin, Benjamin, delegate to convention of 1776: president of convention, 13; support for unicameral legislature, 14

G

Gasoline tax, 142

Geary, James, governor of Pennsylvania (1867-70): message to legislature proposing constitutional revision, 55, 56; Philadelphia election irregularities, 88; pardoning power, alleged abuse of, 76, 77

General Assembly: apportionment, 74; bicameral, 19; powers, 66; procedure, 68, 69; sessions, 67, 144; special legislation prohibited, 65, 66. See also Legislative branch

George, Henry, 51, 52

Governor: appointive powers, 19, 29, 30, 75; budget powers, 133; pardoning power, 19, 75, 76; recommendations of 1959 commission on revision, 151; special session, call of, 19, 75; supervision of administration, 133; tenure and succession, 19, 30, 75, 76, 131, 150, 151; veto power, 19, 75, 133. See also Executive branch

Gowen, Franklin B., delegate to convention of 1872-73, 62, 80, 83, 89, 92, 96, 103, 105

Grange (state): opposition to constitutional revision (1935), 139

Great Works Project, 32, 44

Grundy, Joseph: opposition to constitutional revision (1935), 139

Guffey, Joseph: support for constitutional revision, 140

H

Harrisburg Telegraph: opposition to constitution of 1874, 111, 112, 121; purchase by Cameron interests, 110

Home rule, 132, 155

Hopkinson, Joseph, delegate to convention of 1837, 24, 25

I

Income tax, 3, 137, 141, 153

Incompatibility of offices, 150

Ingersoll, C. J., delegate to convention of 1837, 23; minority report on banks and corporations, 27

Insurance, 41

Iron and steel industry (1860-70), 39-41

Iron-clad oath, 69, 70, 155

J

Judicial branch: constitutional amendments affecting, 31, 32, 129; constitutional provisions, 15, 20, 30, 77, 78;

debates in Council of Censors, 18, convention of 1837, 24, 25, convention of 1872-73, 78-85; recommendations of commissions on revision, 131, 151-53; selection and tenure of judges, 15, 20, 24, 25, 30, 31, 32, 81-85, 129, 151, 152; special provisions for Allegheny County and Philadelphia, 85, 129; structure of court system, 79-81, 129

K

Knight, E. C., delegate to convention of 1872-73, 62, 71, 90, 101, 104

L

Lamberton, Robert A., delegate to convention of 1872-73, 85, 86, 89, 101

League of Women Voters (state): support for constitutional revision, 140

Legislative branch: constitutional amendments affecting, 32, 129, 130, 134, 135, 142, 143, 144; constitutional provisions, 14, 19, 20, 30, 65-68, 70, 74; criticism of in Council of Censors, 18, 19; *debates in convention of 1872-73 on* apportionment of representation, 70-74, biennial sessions, 67, 68, limitations on substantive powers, 66, oath of office, 69, 70, procedure, 68, 69, special legislation, 65, 66, recommendations of commissions on constitutional revision, 131, 137, 149, 150, restoration of annual sessions, 145

Libel, 106, 107

Lieutenant governor: creation of office, 75; member of Board of Pardons, 76

Lilly, William, delegate to convention of 1872-73, 89, 101, 105

M

McAllister, Hugh N., delegate to convention of 1872-73, 67, 92, 93, 103; chairman of committee on elections, 93

McClure, A. K., state senator: *comments on* legislative corruption, 42, 43, registration frauds, 88, social and economic conditions of post-civil war era, 53, 54; *evaluation of* constitution of 1838, 31, 32, constitution of 1874, 124; ratification election, analysis of, 122

MacVeagh, Wayne, delegate to convention of 1872-73, 59, 60, 61, 76; biographical note, 61; chairman of committee on legislation, 63; *remarks on* biennial sessions, 67, big city representation, 71, 72, "iron-clad" oath, 69, problems before convention, 59, selection of judges, 83, signing and numbering of ballots, 91, 92; vote for unlimited succession for governor, 76

Manton, Frank, delegate to convention of 1872-73: remarks on special legislation, 65

Manufacturers (Pennsylvania): employment conditions in (1870), 48-51; growth of (1850-70), 38-40

Meredith, William, delegate to conventions of 1837 and 1872-73, 22, 23, 60, 61, 62, 71, 80; biographical note, 60, 61; president of convention of 1872-73, 62

Metropolitan Plan, 134, 135; recommendation of commission on revision for metropolitan areas, 138

Mifflin, Thomas, delegate to convention of 1789-90, 19

Minor courts, 15, 20, 30, 77, 129, 152, 153

Molly Maguires, 52

Municipal charters, 38, 97, 98; classification amendment, 132; recommendations of commissions on constitutional revision, 137, 138, 155

Municipal debt: amendments affecting, 129, 130, 143; authority borrowing, 141, 145; constitutional limitations, 98, 99; recommendations of commissions on constitutional revision, 131, 154

N

Negro suffrage. *See* Suffrage

O

Optional charter plan, 155

Ordinance of Submission (convention of 1872-73), 64, 118, 120

P

Pennsylvania Bar Association: report on constitutional revision (1935), 139

Pennsylvania Commission on Constitutional revision (1921): appointed, 130; recommendations, 130, 131

Pennsylvania Federation of Labor: support of constitutional revision (1935), 140

Pennsylvania General State Authority, 141, 142

Pennsylvania Manufacturers Association: opposition to constitutional revision (1935), 139

"Pennsylvania Plan," 84, 151, 152

Pennsylvania Railroad Co., 44-47

Pennsylvania State Chamber of Commerce: support for constitutional revision (1921), 132; support withheld (1935), 139

Pennsylvania Turnpike Commission, 141, 142

Pepper, George Wharton, 131, 132

Petroleum production (Pennsylvania), 1860-70, 40

Philadelphia: consolidation of city and county, 70, 143; court provisions, 85, 129; *at mid-nineteenth century*, economic conditions, 49-51, machine control, 54, 87, rivalry with New York City and Baltimore, 43-45; special commissions, 98; recommendations of 1959 commission on constitutional revision, 149; underrepresentation in senate, 70-74

Philadelphia Evening Bulletin, 115

Philadelphia Public Ledger: editorial comments on fee system, 97, libel laws, 107, legislative interference with cities, 98, limited city representation, 73, panic of 1873, 106; support for constitution of 1874, 115, 116, 119

Pickering, Timothy, delegate to convention of 1789-90, 19

Pinchot, Gifford, governor of Pennsylvania (1923-27, 1931-35), 131, 132, 133

Pittsburgh: metropolitan plan amendments, 134, 135; *at mid-nineteenth century*, economic conditions, 49, 50, "ring" politics, 54, special commissions, 98

Pittsburgh Commercial: opposition to constitution of 1874, 110, 111; purchase by Cameron interests, 110

Pittsburgh Evening Chronicle, 114, 115

Pittsburgh Gazette, 42, 47, 59-60, 127; support of constitution of 1874, 112, 113

Pittsburgh Post: editorial comment on libel law, 107; support for constitution of 1874, 112, 113

Pollock, James, governor of Pennsylvania (1855-58), delegate to convention of 1837, 23

Population (Pennsylvania): mid-nineteenth century growth, 52, 53

Porter, James, delegate to convention of 1837, 23, 25

Property values (Pennsylvania), 38

Proprietary party, 10

Provincial conference, 11, 12

Purviance, John N., delegate to convention of 1872-73, 84

Purviance, Samuel A., delegate to conventions of 1837 and 1872-73, 61, 84, 112

Q

Quakers: in Pennsylvania politics, 10, 11, 17

R

Radical Republicans: opposition to constitution of 1874, 109, 110

Railroads: abuses alleged, 46, 47; amendment affecting, 135; *in convention of 1872-73*, railroad article debated, 100-5, railroad influence, 101, 102, railroad representation, 62, triumph of anti-railroad forces, 102, 103; recommendations of 1959 commission on constitutional revision, 155

Real Estate Board of Pennsylvania: support for constitutional revision (1935), 140

Registration: Philadelphia registry law, 87, 109; registration amendment, 128

Rittenhouse, David, delegate to convention of 1776, 13

S

Schnader, William A., 136, 138

Secretary of Commonwealth: appointive officer, 30, 75; member of Board of Pardons, 76; recommendation of 1959 commission on constitutional revision, 151

Sectional differences (Pennsylvania): colonial period, 9-11

Sergeant, John, delegate to convention of 1837, 22; president of convention, 23; support for limited tenure of judges, 25

Smith, William H., delegate to convention of 1872-73, 62, 101

Special assessments, 135

Special legislation: evils of, 55, 56; restrictions on, 65, 66

Special sessions, 19, 75; recommendations of 1959 commission on constitutional revision, 150

Sproul, William C., governor of Pennsylvania (1919-23), 130, 131

Stevens, Thaddeus, delegate to convention of 1837, 23; *remarks on* appointment power of governor, 24, banks and corporations, 28, public education, 29; *position respecting city representation*, 71, office of lieutenant governor, 75, secret societies, 23

Suffrage: colonial, 10; *constitutional provisions* (1776), 14, (1790), 20, (1838), 30, 31, (1874), 92-93; *debates in conventions of 1837 and 1872-73 on* Negro suffrage, 26, 92, property and taxpaying qualifications, 25, 26, 93, 94, residence, 96, woman suffrage, 94-96; recommendations of *commissions on constitutional revision,* 131, 153; residence qualification modified, 145; taxpaying qualification abolished, 135; woman suffrage, 135

Superintendent of Public Instruction: office created, 75; selection, 75, 107, 151

T

Tax Anticipation Act, 139

Tax uniformity clause, 66, 143, 144, 145; recommendations of *commissions on* constitutional revision, 131, 137, 153

Taylor, M. Harvey, 138, 139

U

Unicameral legislature, 14, 19

Urban counties: Allegheny County Metropolitan Plan, 134, 135; Philadelphia city-county consolidation, 70, 143; recommendations of commission on constitutional revision (1935), 138

V

Veterans Bonus: World War I, 134; World War II, 143; Korean conflict, 144

W

Walker, John H., delegate to convention of 1872-73, successor to Meredith as president, 68, 70, 96

Wells v. Bain, et al. and Fitler, et al., 75 Pa. 39 (1873), 118, 119; public reaction to decision, 119, 120

Whigs, 22, 28, 31

White, David N., delegate to convention of 1872-73: opposition to biennial *sessions,* 68; *support for constitution* of 1874, 112

White, Harry, delegate to convention of 1872-73, 57, 60, 63, 116

Wilson, James, delegate to convention of 1789-90, 19

Woman suffrage. See Suffrage

Wood and Owens, et al. v. Quay, in Common Pleas, December term, 1873, 120

Wood's Appeal, 75 Pa. 65 (1874), 120, 121

Woodside, Robert E., chairman of Commission on Constitutional Revision (1959), 148

Woodward, George W., delegate to conventions of 1837 and 1872-73, 23, 61; biographical note, 61; chairman of committee on private corporations (1872-73), 63; *position on* ineligibility of governor to succeed himself, 76, woman suffrage, 94; *remarks on* appointive power of governor, 24, circuit court, 79, 80, corporation, 99, creation of new counties, 97, judiciary, selection and tenure of, 24, 25, 82, limited city representation, 71, viva voce voting, 89

Workmen's Compensation Amendment, 129, 130

Z

Zoning, 131